RECLAIMING YOUR ROOTS

A Self-Healer's Guide to Ancestral Healing Through Transformational Spiritual Practices

BY KRISTEN BLYTHE

Rooted Wisdom Press

Published by Rooted Wisdom Press
Cover design by Kristen Blythe

Paperback ISBN: 978-1-7372917-2-5
Ebook ISBN: 978-1-7372917-3-2

For my soul family.
I love you more than all of creation.

For more publications, companion materials, meditations, courses, and other services from Kristen Blythe, visit:

www.rootedwisdomcoaching.com

Table of Contents

Introduction

Our blood and our bones, they are the fuel and the foundation. Blood circulates through our body one beat at a time, and if we are still and present we can feel the eternal cyclical rhythm of life itself flowing through our veins. Our bones hold us up. They stand upon generation after generation of dust and stone made of the bones of our ancestors, and they remain long after we are gone as the legacy that future generations will stand upon.

In Western culture, we like to think we are our own people made up of our accomplishments, actions, and experiences. While our uniqueness as individuals can't be denied, this separation of our personal identity from the collective ancestral foundation it was built upon is the source of a great spiritual illness that much of humanity suffers from today. This forgetting of our roots separates us from the wisdom and understanding we so greatly need in order to heal on both personal and collective levels. Yet decade after decade, generation after generation, many of us actively work to separate ourselves from the experiences of our ancestors and deny the impact of our past on our present and future.

The blood and the bones paint a different picture, though. They remind us of the interconnectedness of all things. They show us that there is far more to our experience than meets the eye. They anchor the imprint of our past into our physical vessel. They hold us accountable.

We tend to reject or bury the unsavory things in life, but rejection makes things hide, not disappear, and there is always eventually an earthquake or a flood that will bring the buried things to the surface. We can only look the other way for so long before the burdens of generations past can no longer be ignored.

You see, all of those hidden and buried things are part of the foundation that our lives are built upon. When the foundation is out of balance, everything built after it reflects imbalance. Our wars, oppression, inequality, poverty, natural disasters, health challenges, addiction, anxiety, depression, abuse, and trauma are symptoms of a hidden ancestral disease that was seeded in humanity many millennia ago. These imbalances often did not start with us in this lifetime, yet they are part of our world whether we like it or not. The greatest of the challenges we face today have deep roots in the past, but opening our eyes to the past and taking responsibility for its impact on our lives is quite a challenge as well, which is often why we choose to look the other way.

Regardless of what story we tell ourselves about our origins and our responsibility to the past, experiencing challenge is a certainty for us. The question is, then, do we choose the challenge of continuing to bury the past until we bury ourselves along with it, or do we choose the challenge of tending to our roots to create a more healed future for ourselves and future generations?

For those who choose the more sustainable option, a new journey begins here. This journey of ancestral healing ripples throughout time, throughout generations, and throughout humanity. If you close your eyes and sit still for a moment, you'll feel the impact of this simple choice already moving inside you. The choice to look deeper and to heal ignites the process of realigning all parts of yourself and your life to answer the call of your ancestors. This heart-driven choice is the beginning of an alchemical process meant to bring yourself and your lineage into a greater state of truth and wholeness.

Finding our way back to this path of ancestral connection and healing can often be our greatest challenge. When we are not taught about the profound impact our ancestral lineage has on our experience of life by our family or culture, we must start by remembering that this journey exists for us in the first place.

When I reflect on my own path to ancestral healing I have a difficult time pinpointing exactly where it started. I suppose the most truthful answer is that I embarked on this journey long before I stepped into this current life of mine. I come from a soul lineage that has graced me with an attuned intuition, a deep connection with my spirit guides, a compassionate heart, and activated soul wisdom that has come in very handy many times. I was born into a genetic lineage poisoned by sexual and other forms of abuse, and I was the next in line to carry this burden. The deep wounds, trauma, and toxic programming I inherited and experienced through my genetic lineage needed some serious alchemy, and the blessings of my soul lineage have carried me through and allowed me to heal.

Despite my initial blindness to the healing path I was destined to take in this life, I collected breadcrumbs along the way. At age fifteen, a very deep reverence for Celtic spirituality and mysticism awoke within me. No one in my biological family shared this same interest even though my ancestors were of Irish and Scottish descent. Yet, somehow a remembrance of the magic of my lineage suddenly emerged when I was old enough to explore it on my own. Life often leads us to the wisdom we need through our interests, hobbies, and creative inspirations, even if we can't recognize this until hindsight reveals hidden truths.

I have been intuitive my entire life, but I had always been afraid to explore my gifts until my college years afforded me certain freedoms. As a young adult, I finally began to feel brave enough to delve into my more metaphysical interests and abilities. I took my first training in energy healing during the summer of 2000 and my studies in metaphysics, psychic phenomena, and the spirit realms blossomed.

The more I awakened to myself, though, the more I felt and lived with the impact of the abuse I experienced during my childhood. Even though my memory of the most extreme abuse I experienced had been locked away in the hidden vaults of my mind, the impact of trauma remained. Anxiety, depression, autoimmune disease, toxic relationships, isolation, fear, unexplained PTSD, and nervous system dysregulation were an ever-present part of my reality.

Nonetheless, I found a sense of peace, purpose, and balance when I immersed myself in spiritual practice and energy healing. My calling as a healer and intuitive worked as a neutralizing force and coping mechanism for my unexplained imbalances for many years.

Then, one day in my late thirties when the timing was just right, the vault was opened and memories of sexual abuse came flooding back into my mind and body. I thought I had escaped from the ghosts of childhood past and was well into my career as an energy healer when my memories resurfaced. As a result, I was unexpectedly thrown into a maelstrom of personal healing work. Each day consisted of a ruthless regimen of inner alchemy that required every ounce of my physical, mental, emotional, and spiritual strength to get through.

As I fought this inner battle that my ego felt forced into and that my soul had chosen, I very much found myself falling into the realms of darkness that I had worked so hard to escape from for decades. It is in the darkness and in the subconscious layers of our being that we find what is hidden, though. I had left a lot of hidden things behind in my initial efforts to heal from my past prior to the reemergence of my most insidious memories, and returning to the darkness to take a deeper look was not something I ever aspired to do. It was a necessity, though, if I wanted to embody the life I most desired.

I wish I could say that my studies in energy healing and thousands of sessions with clients taught me most of what I know about ancestral healing work. However, it was truly my deep dive into healing my own trauma that led me both into an epic spiritual battle to free myself from the burdens of my genetic ancestral line and to the soul wisdom I needed to create the peaceful and joyful life I so longed for.

Throughout the beginning of my trauma healing process, I truly thought my inner work was just about me and my own inner experience. Exploring the darker places and the hidden things can be very isolating and activating for the ego. It wasn't until after the flashbacks stopped and I felt like my body and mind were somewhat in my control again that I started to view my past experiences with a more neutral eye. I began to use one of my intuitive gifts - the ability to trace imbalances to their origin - to explore my situation a little bit deeper. It was in this place of neutrality that I finally understood that my very personal and painful experiences were never about me at all.

I was born into an ancestral story that began long before I was born. I was at least the third generation in my genetic lineage to experience sexual and other forms of abuse, and the traumas that created the opportunity for this pattern to replicate began even further back. The abuse I experienced was not something that started with me - it was ancestral. I finally realized that in order to fully heal myself from the physical, mental, emotional, and spiritual impact of my childhood experiences, I had to address their ancestral origins. I knew in my bones that although I wasn't responsible for what happened to me, as a member of my lineage carrying the energies of abuse, it was my responsibility to do everything in my power to end the cycle.

It was shortly after this revelatory experience that my spirit guides taught me about the ancestral energetic template that informs each life we live, the energies contained within it, and the methods I could use to overcome the ancestral burdens and personal traumas that had plagued me for decades. I learned that the shape my external life and inner landscape took were intrinsically connected to the ancestral energies I inherited. With this revelation, my personal healing journey became ancestral healing very quickly.

I began referring to this energetic template as the Ancestral Blueprint™, and I started working with its energies within my own being to continue healing. Healing myself meant reaching beyond myself into the past, into my roots, and into all that existed before me. It is the most accessible of the methods I learned through my own ancestral healing work that I share with you here as we move forward on this healing journey together.

My ancestral background is rooted in the traditions of Celtic spirituality, yet I have also learned from teachers of many different traditional practices including those from Tibetan Buddhism, Toltec shamanism, Rosicrucianism, Hawaiian mysticism, and other spiritual and healing traditions from around the world. Over the years I have found that it can sometimes feel uncomfortable and even difficult to attempt healing work through the lens of an unfamiliar cultural or spiritual tradition. It can also feel equally as difficult to connect with our own ancestral traditions when our family of origin or the modern society we live in do not have an integrated practice of doing so.

Many of us have become so disconnected from our roots that when we finally begin to look at them, we feel completely lost and struggle to find a way to reconnect. Sometimes we explore unfamiliar practices that might feel very awkward to us. In other cases, we might try to reconnect with our own forgotten ancestral traditions which can be a very isolating journey in our modern world. Regardless of how we choose to begin exploring our ancestral roots, we all have ancient ancestral lineages to draw from, both through our genetic connections and our spiritual connections.

While there is much value in accessing ancestral healing through the traditions of the past, there is equally as much value in developing new techniques that are accessible in a modern era where many people are unaware of or are disconnected from their ancestral origins and traditions. The practices and teachings you will find here are meant to be used independently of any specific tradition, and are also designed to be applied to any existing spiritual practices or traditions that you prefer to work through. Modern techniques with ancient roots is how we will proceed, as I find that this is the most flexible and inclusive path forward for all.

One of the greatest lessons I integrated in the aftermath of my personal crucible of ancestral healing is that no one out there beyond myself could have done my work for me. I also knew that moving forward, if I were to be in my integrity, the only way I could truly help others as a healer was to guide others to be the best self-healers they could be. After I emerged from my cocoon of healing, my newly claimed mission was to support others in revealing their own personal truth using the intuitive gifts and healing knowledge I had gained along my path. I had finally learned how to embrace the true path of the healer that so many understand intellectually, but fail to honor in practice. I consider myself more of a guide and a teacher now, and it is these roles that have truly brought me back to myself in a way that years of hands-on energy healing work never quite accomplished.

As a teacher, I see it as my job to share knowledge that I have gathered along my path in a format that is accessible and allows you to apply it to your own life, regardless of your cultural background, spiritual traditions, or personal growth practices. I use language throughout this book that is familiar to me, but by all means, substitute my terminology with your own, add your own flair and style, and expand upon these practices in any way that honors your traditions and your lineage. My way has worked for me and countless clients I have worked with, yet it is not the only way. There are many ways to approach healing, and I trust that you will keep what resonates and discard the rest.

Your job is to trust yourself, trust the process, and know that you are your own most powerful healer, for you are the only one with access to the experiences, energies, and wisdom contained in your unique Ancestral Blueprint. We always have the exact gifts and resources that are needed to balance and transform our ancestral burdens into a healed expression within ourselves. This inherent divine balance in our Ancestral Blueprint provides us with everything we need to uplift ourselves and overcome past challenges with perfect timing.

Your healing work is yours and yours alone, but it does not have to be done alone. While no healer, intuitive, counselor, or spiritual leader can do this work for you, it is always helpful to have wisdom from experience and support by your side when you begin this work. As you forge ahead and begin learning how to work with your Ancestral Blueprint to heal and create the life you desire, know that there is no rush. Take your time digesting this information, work through healing at a gentle pace, gather a team of physical and spiritual support around you, and always follow your heart and internal guidance system as your primary compass.

As we embark on this healing journey together, know that your healed ancestors are with you, your spirit guides are with you, Spirit is with you, and the highest version of yourself is with you. They cheer you on, support you, assist you, uplift you as you do this work, and they do so for your highest good and the highest good of all creation.

While healing is challenging, this is a challenge that is supported and guided. It is a challenge that allows for grace to step in whenever the lifting gets too heavy, and it is a challenge that leads to beautiful transformation and upliftment. This is the work you were born for, and it begins here.

Part I

Foundations of Ancestral Healing

Chapter 1

Exploring the Ancestral Blueprint

I magine for a moment that you are an architect with an impressive resume and an exciting new job. You landed this job because you have a specific set of skills and experience that are needed for a very complex and ancient project. This is a project that has been in the works for many thousands of years, and countless other architects have had a hand in creating it. Some of these architects were brilliant and offered their wisdom and unique genius to the project. Others were not so helpful and left a bit of a mess in their wake.

You accepted this new job because you knew it would be a challenge and that it would help you develop your skills and knowledge as an architect. You also know that when your time on this project ends you'll have made a significant contribution both to the project and to your own personal growth. This is no ordinary job. This is the project of a lifetime with a legacy older than time.

You show up in your assigned office and carry in boxes full of your personal notes, research, and plans for the project, but you notice that the room is already stacked full of boxes labeled with the names of those who came before you. On your desk sits a blueprint for the structure that is being built, and you look out your office window to see a portion of this structure taking shape outside. You realize that the building you stand in is the project itself, and it looks nothing like you thought it would. You look around the room and notice that the ceiling is leaking in the corner and there are a few cracks in the walls. You sigh as you realize that your experience here is going to be directly impacted by what was left behind by those who came before you.

The building matches the blueprint on your desk exactly. Some parts of the structure are fully functional, beautiful, and serve a unique purpose for the community and those who built it. Other parts of this structure are in disrepair, a bit outdated, and in need of renovation. There are even a few sections here and there that are nothing more than a pile of rubble. These sections need a bulldozer and a new design altogether. You look down at the blueprint in front of you and know that each change you make will directly impact the structure of this building, yourself, and everyone else connected to this project.

You pull your own designs out of the boxes you brought in and begin comparing them to the blueprint. Excitement moves through you as you notice that the blueprint contains a brilliant solution to a structural problem you were having a hard time addressing in your own plans. This initial excitement wanes a bit, though, when you notice that there's no way that the existing blueprint can accommodate other ideas that you had hoped to build. It's going to take a lot of work to integrate your own inspirations and aspirations into this incredibly tremendous project and repair the damage left behind by some of the architects that came before you. You're perfect for the task though, and you have the support of upper management and the wisdom of your predecessors on your side.

Just as the expert architect steps into a new project armed

with their training, experience, and unique creative expression, we step into each lifetime carrying the skills, wisdom, and imprint of our past experiences with us, along with our own challenges, traumas, and limitations. We are a unique expression of energy that has been shaped by all we have experienced in our soul's infinite journey. Each lifetime gives us an opportunity to continue that journey in an ancestral project that has its own challenges and assets.

The combination of this ancestral project we enter into through our genetic lineage and our own personal project that comes in the form of our soul's energies and their evolution, together create the unique physical experience that we have in each lifetime. When we enter our physical body, these two projects become singular and inseparable within us. We then begin a process of transformation for ourselves and the genetic lineage we are born into that cannot be replicated under any other condition.

❧

YOUR UNIQUE TEMPLATE

While our physical bodies are the zero-point of transformation for the genetic and soul ancestral projects that coalesce within us, all things physical consist of and are informed by energy first. Just as a physical building needs an architectural blueprint before it can be built, our physical experience is formed by energy that moves through energetic templates. These energetic templates exist all around us and within our own energy field. They program and direct energy into a specific form ranging from the spiritual to the physical.

The energetic template created by our genetic and soul lineages combining within us is called our Ancestral Blueprint. It exists within our personal energy field, therefore Ancestral Blueprint work and ancestral healing are forms of energy healing. This is energy healing on the deepest of levels, as Ancestral Blueprint work gets to the root of everything we experience that springs from our past, heals it at its core, and transforms our inner landscape and physical life experience in the process.

Our Ancestral Blueprint consists of a combination of energies we inherit through our entire personal ancestral lineage. These energies include our genetic ancestral lineage made up of our biological relatives, and our soul's ancestral lineage which contains our past soul experiences and our soul connections. The unification of these two separate lineages in an individual is distinctive and unique. Like an energetic fingerprint, there is no other person that has ever existed who has the same Ancestral Blueprint that you have in this lifetime.

Our inheritances from our soul's lineage and the lineage of our genetic ancestors combine within us. They inform each other, alter each other, and together create our Ancestral Blueprint. This Ancestral Blueprint is complex, multi-layered, and consists of many different facets of information. It is the primary energetic template that informs the manifestation of all aspects of our lives - physical, mental, emotional, energetic, and spiritual. Likewise, our intentions, choices, and actions transform our Ancestral Blueprint in new ways each moment of each day. Once we incarnate, our entire life becomes a process of transformation that is informed by this matrix of ever-changing energetic data. This fundamental energetic template shapes the core of our physical experience, for better or worse.

Our Ancestral Blueprint is full of burdens and gifts. The burdens stem from unresolved personal and ancestral traumas, the limiting patterns and intentions we have adopted and replicated that are a far cry from our soul's truth, and the manifestations of these core imbalances. Ancestral gifts come in many forms as well, from ancestral knowledge and soul wisdom to physical aptitudes and abilities to supportive connections on physical and non-physical levels.

We enter life physically through a genetic lineage that contains its own story, its own structure, its own wisdom, and its own imprint of past experiences. This physical avenue for experience allows us to develop our own energy in new ways, learn in new ways, and it offers us an opportunity to contribute our unique energy to everyone and everything we touch in our physical lives. Our genetic ancestral energy stream consists of a combination of the life experiences, choices, and intentions of all of our genetically related ancestors. This means that we directly energetically inherit through our genetic lineage both the limitations and assets of all our blood relatives.

Our embodiment within a genetic lineage also has a permanent impact on the lineage and everyone who has ever been and ever will be a part of it. The energies we create in a genetic lineage, both balanced and unbalanced, leave their mark. All of our biological relations, in one way or another, have to deal with that impact. In some cases, this means they will repeat the patterns and suffer the effect of the traumas, limiting beliefs, and limiting intentions that we experience in our lifetime. In other cases, this means they will benefit from the wisdom, balance, and gifts we leave for future generations to build a life upon. In most cases, it's a bit of both.

When we exit each life, the experiences we've had create eternal change. The version of us that is represented by a single lifetime's Ancestral Blueprint is permanently encoded into our soul, and we carry the balances, imbalances, growth, learning, and connections created through each life with us. Each life we live and each genetic lineage we incarnate into become permanent parts of who we are.

Regardless of how we each choose to shape the legacy we leave behind for future generations, we have to be aware that this legacy did not start with us, nor will it end with us. We are a singular part of an infinite picture. We have blessings to offer our lineage and we have things to heal. Our genetic lineage has gifts to offer us and has imbalances that need balancing. This marriage of lineages within us creates a give-and-take dynamic. The question is, what are we giving and what are we taking?

If we are alive, whether we are aware of it or not, we are doing Ancestral Blueprint work. While our soul lineage energies expand with each life we live, genetic ancestral streams expand with each new individual that is born into the lineage and with the experiences they have. Every choice we make, every action we take, and every intention we hold all change the shape of our Ancestral Blueprint. If we do these things unconsciously and without self-awareness, we are likely feeling, thinking, and manifesting our lives through the limitations and burdens that exist in our Ancestral Blueprint. If we are aware and aligned with our soul's truth, we can identify the imbalances in our Ancestral Blueprint and do the work necessary to shift these imbalances into something that honors our own unique soul expression. The more healing work we do within our Ancestral Blueprint, the more of our authentic soul-self we can bring forth into our physical lives.

The soul lineage aspect of our Ancestral Blueprint consists of the ancestral memory of all of our experiences as a soul. It contains the imprint of everything we have personally experienced, and it anchors the effects of these experiences into our life as well. This includes any unhealed traumas, limiting beliefs, and patterns from our past, as well as any soul wisdom, skills, gifts, and healed patterning we have achieved throughout our existence.

Everything we learn through exploring the soul lineage aspect of our Ancestral Blueprint is simply a remembrance of what has already been. This remembrance, no matter what form it comes in or how conscious it is, gives us the opportunity to alchemize the more dense energies in our Ancestral Blueprint into soul skills, wisdom, and balance.

Regardless of our conscious understanding of our soul's

history, our Ancestral Blueprint as it exists in the present moment contains the most information it has ever had, and we are constantly adding to it with each experience. In each moment of our current life, we are always at our most advanced state on a soul level, regardless of how things may appear to us physically.

Our soul energies are part of us and cannot be taken away; however, there are many limitations that prevent the full scope of who we are from entering physicality. We are multidimensional beings, and some aspects of who we are can only exist on the level of Spirit and cannot manifest into physical form. Sometimes different expressions of our soul can exist harmoniously in higher realms, but cannot coexist simultaneously in our dense, linear physical reality. In other cases, the ancestral burdens we inherit or incarnation agreements that we make through our genetic lineage prevent some of our soul expressions from coming through. With healing, we can access and embody many of these soul lineage energies as we progress through life, especially if the soul skills and wisdom we possess would be beneficial to us and our mission here.

Ancestral healing of our soul lineage involves working with past lives and soul connections to heal trauma and patterns that are imprinted in our Ancestral Blueprint. We can heal from past life traumas and wounds through our normal life experiences and challenges, regardless of our understanding, belief, or awareness of past lives; however, actively working with past lives and other aspects of ourselves can rapidly accelerate healing and growth.

The term *past lives* refers to lives that we have already experienced, and not necessarily lives in the chronological past. We have all had countless lifetimes in many realms, dimensions, times, and planes of existence, some of which may have been in our chronological future or in a dimension where time does not exist as we understand it.

Additionally, our physical expression in each lifetime can be very different. We are not necessarily the same gender, race, sexual orientation, or even species in other lifetimes, so working with our soul's lineage can very much expand our understanding of ourselves and who we are. The illusion of separation begins to fade away as we explore the multidimensional aspects of ourselves and our connection to all that exists.

While much of the energetic data we inherit through our soul lineage and genetic lineage energy streams is separate, there can be some crossover between them. We could potentially have incarnated into our current genetic lineage at a different time in another life. It is also possible for us to have incarnated with some of the souls that currently exist in our genetic lineage in a different genetic lineage with different relationships altogether in a past life. Our child could have been our parent, a sibling, a friend, a boss, or an uncle for example. This leads to a crossover of information between our soul and genetic energy streams in certain areas of our Ancestral Blueprint. These crossover points are often where a greater opportunity for balancing exists. The energies in these areas of our Ancestral Blueprint are strengthened, and therefore bring any themes related to these crossover points to our attention.

The work of ancestral healing is self-healing, for all of the information we need to take up this task exists within our own personal Ancestral Blueprint. The contents of our Ancestral Blueprint are reflected in many ways in our personal life experiences. Our experiences hold the key to unlocking the secrets of this unique energetic template. Once unlocked, we have the power to balance and complete the cycles that were left unbalanced and incomplete by our ancestors.

We tend to think of physicality and energy as completely separate worlds, yet the more I do this work, the more I witness the energetic and the physical in an inseparable dance that creates all that we experience in life. We cannot have physicality without an energetic counterpart, for it is the energy that creates all things, connects all things, and moves all things into manifestation. This is why when we approach ancestral healing work through the lens of energy, it does not matter whether we physically know our genetic relatives, their story, or their origins. It is the energy that connects us, not our physical relationships or genealogical knowledge. Ancestral healing is for everyone, regardless of life circumstances, and the information needed to heal the wounds of our lineage is all there encoded into our being.

Our Ancestral Blueprint can be completely transformed without a physical connection to others in our lineage. This work begins and ends within each of us. It is internal work. There is no need to remain in toxic relationships, expose ourselves to abuse, find our long-lost relatives, or make things look a certain way in our external world. If we can connect with our heart, we can heal. The heart is where we access our truth.

As we do this internal work, our Ancestral Blueprint shifts and changes. The traumas and limiting beliefs of the past that inform our life experiences transform into wisdom, love, peace, and truth. Our reality then begins to reflect the most authentic version of us that is no longer influenced by the limitations of those who came before us or our own limiting past experiences. This work leads to rapid and significant upliftment and personal transformation, for it addresses the core templates that our entire life is built upon.

The beauty here is that this healing isn't just about self-healing either. Our Ancestral Blueprints may be unique to each of us, but they are connected to all of the other individuals and Ancestral Blueprints within our lineage on a quantum energetic level. When we work to heal the imbalances influencing our personal Ancestral Blueprint, this healing is accessible to every person in our lineage through the connections that exist within the template itself. Ancestral healing is a transformational process that occurs on a very personal and internal level, that consequently has an infinite healing effect on everyone and everything we have ever been connected to in any lifetime. That's some pretty powerful stuff!

When we work within our Ancestral Blueprint on an energetic level to make shifts and heal trauma, this can have a very real physical effect on our DNA, and consequently our health and physical wellness. Epigenetics is the study of how environmental, behavioral, psychological, and experiential factors influence the expression of our DNA. Epigenetic changes do not alter the structure of our physical DNA, but they can affect whether our existing gene sequences are turned on or off. While we may have physical DNA that has the potential to express itself in certain ways, external factors such as diet, exercise, environment, trauma, emotions, and a variety of other influences can determine whether these potentials become a reality or not.

Additionally, epigenetic changes are frequently reversible, so when we change certain behaviors and do our healing, we can fundamentally change the way our DNA expresses. This means that the spiritual, mental, and emotional shifts that we make through ancestral healing work, or really any form of personal growth work, can have a very real impact on how our physical body behaves and reacts to the world around us. With this in mind, I would argue that there are many physical conditions that are impossible to permanently transform for the better without addressing the ancestral roots of the imbalances that created these conditions in the first place.

Tending to our roots is exactly what we are doing when we begin the journey of ancestral healing, and it is a very fruitful journey when we think of the far-reaching impact of this process. Healing the problems that plague humanity seems impossible and overwhelming when we try to tackle the big picture all at once, yet we each have access to a small piece of the big picture that is intrinsically connected to all of the other pieces of that picture. As we begin to work within our personal Ancestral Blueprint - the piece of the big picture that belongs to us alone - we pass any healing we achieve down to our children, nieces, nephews, their children, and so on down the line. We also pass this healing to our future lifetimes where we will not have to repeat the limiting patterns of our current life once they are balanced.

On an energetic level, we offer this healing to our ancestors and genetic relations as well, as the healing we do within our Ancestral Blueprint is available to all of our relations - past, present, and future - through energetic connections. When enough of us take up this work, our future, the future of our lineage, and the future of humanity begin to take shape in a new way. As above, so below. As within, so without. The work we do internally is how we shape the world around us into something better.

✍

LINEAGE COMPATIBILITY

The more we explore the structure of our Ancestral Blueprint and its energies, it becomes clear that our lives are created through a unique relationship between two separate histories. Change and transformation occur through this unification of lineages within us, both internally and outside of ourselves. We can often understand our relationship to our own soul's experiences and our ever-expanding journey through the cosmos, but we might start to wonder how we end up in the genetic lineage we incarnate into in each lifetime. This may be especially true if we have experienced a lot of trauma as a result of being in our particular genetic lineage.

One of the four primary reasons we incarnate into a genetic lineage is to create the opportunities we need for soul growth.

Genetic lineages are chosen because they have specific programming, dynamics, traumas, or abilities that create the circumstances that best align us with our highest path of growth as a soul. Opportunities for growth through our genetic lineage do not necessarily always feel good or feel like growth, but they do allow for growth nonetheless. We might incarnate into a lineage because challenges we experience as a child and the process of overcoming those challenges allow us to learn new ways to navigate conflict. We might struggle as a soul to understand boundaries, and we incarnate into a lineage that teaches us how to set and maintain healthy boundaries. We might have a desire as a soul to learn how to express ourselves artistically, so we incarnate into a lineage of artists who can teach us. Our genetic lineage always offers us something that will help us develop on a soul level.

We may also choose our genetic lineage for the purpose of balancing ancestral burdens. Our genetic lineage may offer us opportunities to balance our soul energies, and so we might incarnate into a family that can help us balance soul lineage ancestral burdens created in other lifetimes. We might also incarnate with specific individuals in a genetic lineage to balance any ancestral burdens from other lifetimes that involved these individuals. When we incarnate into a lineage, we can also offer our soul gifts and skills to help the genetic lineage overcome some of its burdens. As a result, we stop the cycle of passing those burdens down the line. Likewise, our genetic lineage offers us certain perspectives, templates, skills, and other gifts that can help us to develop as a soul in ways that create more balance for us.

The genetic compatibility of our biological family is another reason we incarnate into a certain genetic lineage. We all have specific skills and wisdom that need to be expressed in a lifetime to fulfill our mission or purpose. In order for this to be possible, we need to incarnate into a lineage that has the genetic predisposition for certain traits so that we can access or develop the abilities and skills that we need for a given life. For example, if we are meant to be a good singer we will need a body that can physically sing well. Incarnating into a genetic lineage that can offer the genes for a good set of vocal cords may be an important reason to choose a genetic lineage.

Finally, our genetic lineage is often chosen because it provides us with opportunities or support that aid us in fulfilling our mission in each lifetime. This may be through challenges we experience with our genetic family, it may be through the absence of connection with a genetic family, or it may be through the love, support, and nurturance of our genetic family. Ultimately, no matter what our interactions with our genetic relations are, incarnating into a lineage provides us with the opportunities we need to fulfill our purpose and soul mission in each life.

When we select a genetic lineage before we incarnate, we encode the big plans we have for our life into our personal soul contract. Soul contracts are agreements that we make before each incarnation to have certain experiences that will benefit our soul's growth in each life. Our soul contract can include agreements with people from past lives, soul family, genetic family, and even individuals we have never encountered before that may create a certain experience for us that we can benefit from. These agreements are meant to give us opportunities to resolve or balance any imbalances that we may have in our energy, help us fulfill our soul mission, and create experiences for us that help us learn and grow.

Our soul contract works through our Ancestral Blueprint in that it highlights the areas of our Ancestral Blueprint that can be balanced in each lifetime and contractualizes the opportunity to do so. This means that our soul contract is designed to create balance and growth through each lifetime, both for ourselves and our genetic lineage.

The coming together of our soul lineage and genetic lineage through incarnation gives us the unique opportunity to balance energies for both energy streams. Each lineage provides certain templates, skills, support, connections, and wisdom that can assist with balancing aspects of the other, although the amount of balancing needed in each lineage is not necessarily equally weighted.

Part of our soul contract involves the genetic lineage we will incarnate into, and we choose our genetic family as a foundational part of our soul contract before we incarnate. This choice is made at a soul level as a co-creation with our higher self and guides, not at the level of our human personality. Before we incarnate, there are agreements made between ourselves and the other members of our genetic lineage that allow us to enter the family lineage at birth through our chosen parents. Additionally, we choose the majority of circumstances that we incarnate into including those surrounding our birth process, whether or not we will stay with our birth family, and even any health challenges and physical features we may be born with. As soon as the two aspects of our Ancestral Blueprint come together through our incarnation into a genetic family, the transformation of both of our ancestral lines begins. This transformation continues throughout our life as we have experiences and make different choices.

It is important to remember that while we may choose our family before we incarnate, we are never responsible for any harm or abuse we suffer as a result of family connections or relationships. When we create and agree to our soul contracts, we may know that there are predispositions for certain behaviors or actions with each person we are connected to, but each individual is responsible for their own actions, and these actions are not always guaranteed before incarnation. We may grow through challenging experiences; however, recognizing and leaving abusive relationships and healing their impact is often the best path forward for balancing ancestral burdens.

It is very important to recognize that there is a difference between abusive, toxic, and trauma-inducing relationships and challenging or triggering relationships. It can be critical to our healing and growth to not perpetuate relationships that are abusive or create trauma for us, as these relationships limit our sovereignty and often create more imbalance that we will eventually need to heal. We often have other relationships that are contentious, challenging, or occasionally triggering. These relationships are important as they can lead to the most growth as long as both individuals are respectful and attempt to grow and heal when conflict arises. Ultimately, we are never required to maintain toxic or abusive relationships in order to heal or balance our ancestral burdens. It is important to recognize where these types of relationships exist in our lives and navigate them in a way that is safe for us.

The ultimate function of our soul contract is to help us learn and grow, and once the learning and growth that were meant to come from contracted experiences or relationships have occurred, we no longer need those relationships or experiences. It is important to know that we are sovereign beings with free will, and we can learn to navigate our soul contract and Ancestral Blueprint in a beneficial and uplifting way rather than feeling bound to toxic relationships or experiences.

೭౨

THE RIPPLE EFFECT

Part of working with and balancing our Ancestral Blueprint is recognizing that we are the zero-point of responsibility. We are responsible for our own unique Ancestral Blueprint and any energies or patterns anchored into our experience by it, regardless of where they came from. This means that we are all responsible for healing our own trauma and limiting patterns so that they do not impact future generations. It also means that we are responsible for removing or transforming any limiting energies in our energy field that affect us through either of our ancestral lineages, even if they did not originate from us. If something is part of our reality and impacts our experience, we have a responsibility to it. What affects us is always in our experience for a reason.

By balancing ancestral burdens and restoring natural order to our being, we create a ripple effect throughout our entire Ancestral Blueprint. Any changes in our own Ancestral Blueprint impact those who are connected to us through either of our ancestral lines. Healing ourselves is our responsibility alone and does not require the permission or awareness of others, yet it can have a profound positive impact on others just the same.

We can acknowledge that the positive choices we make and actions we take have a direct physical impact on the individuals in our family, whether they are blood-related or not, because our choices and actions affect others. In a very real way, the ripple effect of our healing can be witnessed by our living connections as we begin behaving in different ways and attracting new experiences. When we choose to shift a pattern in ourselves to something different than what was taught to us by our parents or grandparents, and then teach that new pattern to our children, we directly affect the patterns in our lineage. Likewise, if past generations witness changes we make in our lives that conflict with or are outside of their understanding, we expose them to new ideas and ways of living. This does not mean that these individuals will change, but at the very least, we are bringing attention to alternative ideas and ways of being that our relatives may be blind to.

Through our actions, we provide opportunities for others around us to make different choices. We bring their awareness to patterns, traumas, and beliefs that exist for them by creating contrast between their way and our own way. When we are exposed to contrast, we are often forced to either make changes or double down on our old patterns. Regardless of what our connections choose, witnessing our healing offers them a choice that they were perhaps not previously aware of.

This same concept applies to energy healing, but working on the energetic level has a much broader reach than the physical changes we make. With ancestral healing, we do not need to be physically connected to or know anything about anyone in our genetic lineage to heal ourselves or to affect our lineage. Our responsibility lies within us to do the healing we desire for ourselves, and this healing makes an energetic imprint on our genetic lineage through our Ancestral Blueprint. It affects our ancestors and future generations regardless of how we are or are not connected to them.

If we begin to consider the far-reaching effect that our personal ancestral healing journey can have on others through our Ancestral Blueprint, it becomes very clear that Ancestral Blueprint work is profound. The number of direct genetic ancestors we have doubles with each generation back. By the time we reach ten generations behind us, our healing work reaches at least 2,046 individuals besides ourselves. Expand that to twenty generations back and we have over two million individuals that our personal healing work directly impacts energetically.

This might not seem to matter since most of these individuals lived long ago until we consider reincarnation. The healing we offer to our genetic ancestors through our Ancestral Blueprint travels with them through any future lifetimes they have, which impacts all of the future genetic lineages they will incarnate into. If we expand our thinking a bit and consider how many future lifetimes we are positively impacting energetically by balancing our Ancestral Blueprint within ourselves, the number is astronomical. We could pass a person on the street that was once our great-great-great-great-grandfather and the healing we are doing could be positively impacting that person and whatever genetic lineage they are now incarnated into. The internal work we do for ourselves to balance our Ancestral Blueprint truly impacts all of humanity.

Despite the significant energetic impact of Ancestral Blueprint work, not all of our ancestors will choose to accept the healing that is offered to them. When we heal our Ancestral Blueprint, we heal the templates within our own personal Ancestral Blueprint. These new balanced templates are then available to those we are connected to should they choose to accept them. Some of our connections will choose to accept these new balanced templates into their own Ancestral Blueprint, others will not choose to accept the healing for one reason or another. It is never our job to force healing onto others, for everyone has free will and is on their own journey. By balancing our own Ancestral Blueprint, though, we are offering a new opportunity for others to rapidly heal and grow.

If the higher self of one of our ancestors chooses to accept the new balanced template that we have created through our healing, a new imprint representing this balancing will appear in their own Ancestral Blueprint. This energetic imprint serves as a catalyst for the individual to begin releasing any imbalances and energies that are not in alignment with this newly healed template. To aid this release, circumstances, opportunities, and experiences will coalesce for them to complete the energetic balancing. It can take time for this process to occur, yet once a healed template is accepted by the higher self of anyone, the process begins to unfold in a way that serves their highest good.

When we work toward balancing our Ancestral Blueprint, we may notice changes in the living ancestors we are still connected to. They may make sudden and profound shifts, attract opportunities to finally heal what they have been avoiding for a long time, and grow in ways that would not have been possible prior to our own healing work. Our living ancestors do not even need to be consciously aware of the healing we are doing for ourselves for it to work for both us and them. As long as their higher self chooses to accept any balanced templates that we have created in our own Ancestral Blueprint, healing will take place.

The healing our ancestors choose will unfold in perfect timing for them. While it is not our responsibility to oversee this healing, observing positive changes in our own lives and for those we are connected to due to our personal healing process can be very exciting and uplifting.

Our healed templates are naturally available to those we are connected to through our Ancestral Blueprint. However, consciously offering these templates to our lineage increases the impact of our work. We can use the power of our conscious awareness of limiting patterns in our Ancestral Blueprint and our healing of these patterns to offer this same healing to any of our ancestors who would like to accept it. Giving specific permission to our guides and Spirit to offer healing to our lineage through our Ancestral Blueprint can greatly amplify and accelerate this process. This can be done with a simple statement out loud or in your mind similar to the following:

I give permission to my guides, higher self, and Spirit to offer any healed templates and balanced energies that exist in my Ancestral Blueprint to all of my soul and genetic relations. As a representative of my ancestral lineages, I give permission for healing to commence for both of my lineages that is in alignment with my healed templates, honors the free will choices of my ancestors and descendants, and that serves the highest good of all creation.

This statement opens opportunities for healing to pass through your lineage without interacting with your ancestors yourself. Our only true responsibility when it comes to healing is ourselves, and it is not our responsibility to undertake healing that belongs to others. We have enough work on our plate to balance our own Ancestral Blueprint, so attempting to do this work for others is often biting off more than we are meant to chew.

This healing of our lineage is, instead, an offering and opening of avenues to heal. This would be like creating our own recipe, baking and eating our own bread, and offering our recipe to the family. By making this offering, we are honoring the free will and choices of our ancestors while also giving a great gift to those who would like to accept it. Our ancestors will need to do their own baking, as their own growth comes from learning to bake the bread themselves, but having the recipe helps greatly, and a lot more bread will come of it.

We attract every aspect of our lives through the energies that are contained within our whole being. We are perhaps most familiar with how our thoughts, emotions, and intentions can manifest our physical experience, but there are many more energies that impact the things we manifest and experience in life. Our Ancestral Blueprint is made of energy, and so are the traumas, limiting beliefs, limiting intentions, and other unbalanced ancestral energies that are anchored into our being by our Ancestral Blueprint. Our balanced emotions, belief templates, patterns, and other energies also attract experiences to us. This means that working to balance our Ancestral Blueprint and releasing toxic energies and patterns through this work will also completely change what we magnetize to us in life for the better. For some individuals, the majority of their life circumstances are attracted through unbalanced ancestral energies, so doing this work can be extremely fruitful and can lead to significant positive change.

Ancestral healing work is ultimately about ending the cycle of passing ancestral burdens down through our lineage by working with these patterns in our own Ancestral Blueprint. This means that as we do this work, we break toxic patterns within ourselves and ensure that these patterns and dense energies do not repeat or expand through us. With this as our intention, we move forth with a new awareness of our role and a heightened sense of responsibility to ourselves and our ancestors.

Chapter 2

Ancestral Burdens

A s the architect in charge of our Ancestral Blueprint and the structures built from it, it is our job to explore the templates and energies that exist in our Ancestral Blueprint and to transform them in ways that feel aligned with us as an individual. Many of the ancestral energies we inherit from our genetic lineage, and even energies that we bring with us through our soul experiences, are not reflective of our most authentic expression. These limiting energies in our Ancestral Blueprint act as blocks to our upliftment, well-being, and fulfillment in life. They are what hold us back from our mission and purpose, keep us feeling stuck, and leave us feeling poorly about ourselves and our lives.

The limiting energies in our Ancestral Blueprint are called *ancestral burdens*. These ancestral burdens are inherited energies that stem from the imbalances in our ancestral lineages. They impact us and everyone we are connected to through our Ancestral Blueprint in limiting or harmful ways. Life is not isolated. It is cyclical and eternal. The intentions, choices, and actions of the past impact more than just the individual who created them. They have a lasting ripple effect that is often felt for many generations.

While the actions of the past influence every single moment we experience, our current actions and choices influence the trajectory of past actions and how they will affect our future experiences. This means that while the actions of our ancestors and the experiences of our own past shape our present experience, we can choose at any moment to take an action that will completely transform our experience into a more balanced state. We are never truly victims of the past, for although the effects of extremely unbalanced actions can be painful and challenging, balancing an unbalanced past can be done in an instant with a bit of understanding and conscious loving action.

Healing our ancestral burdens requires taking action in our own lives to transform the impact of our ancestors' unbalanced energies on our current reality. When we balance ancestral burdens, we shift influential energies from our lineage that are not in alignment with our most loving and unified expression into energies that are reflective of our most authentic self. The more in alignment we are with our authentic self or our soul-self in all of our intentions, choices, and actions, whether they are conscious or unconscious, the more we free ourselves from our inherited ancestral burdens. The result of this work is always learning, growth, and healing in some form.

Ancestral healing work is all about empowering ourselves as sovereign beings over our life path, rather than becoming the victim of energies affecting us that were created by our genetic ancestors or through past life experiences we have had. There is no need to repeat the same patterns over and over again when we learn the proper methods to shift these patterns and commit to our own loving and balanced path. There are many ways that ancestral burdens can manifest in our lineage, and each manifestation of them can be addressed in specific ways once we become aware of how we are being affected by them.

There are three primary types of ancestral burdens that we can have in our Ancestral Blueprint, and each has a very specific impact on the way we experience life. The different forms of ancestral burdens that we have are connected and related to each other, and working with one specific form of burden can help us identify and release others. This relationship between our ancestral burdens can allow us to quickly release entire groups of blocks and limitations we experience at one time.

❧

ANCESTRAL TRAUMA

The first form of ancestral burden that we carry in our Ancestral Blueprint is ancestral trauma, which is the most impactful form of ancestral burden. Just as we have each experienced trauma in life, many of our ancestors and past life selves experienced trauma as well. If those traumas and their effect are never fully healed in a lineage, the energies and patterns created by those traumas can be passed down to us both through physical interaction with our relatives and through our Ancestral Blueprint. This means that we may be experiencing challenging patterns, emotional imbalances, toxic relationship dynamics, or even health challenges as a result of trauma that originated from somewhere in our ancestral lineage. This is the case even if we have never even met our biological family members or have no awareness of our past lives.

Ancestral traumas come in two forms, the first being collective traumas. These are any traumatic experiences that our ancestors had as a result of a collective human experience. These collective experiences could have been on a global level or a more localized level; however, they would have been experiences that were not unique within the family or to a certain individual. War, famine, political or cultural oppression, pandemics, and environmental disasters are just some examples of collective trauma. These types of events have a far-reaching impact on those who experience them, yet each individual experiences and is affected by these traumatic events in unique ways based on their specific circumstances.

The Great Depression is a well-known example of a collective trauma that has burdened lineages all over the world, and was even personally experienced by many of our elders who are still living today. Many of the limiting patterns that people struggle to shift associated with abundance, security, work, and other related themes often originate from the trauma their lineage experienced during the Great Depression. People who have never struggled financially their entire lives may penny-pinch and hoard resources, never throw anything away, or feel obligated to eat everything on their plate because of an unconscious ancestral imprint of trauma. In others, this same ancestral imprint may cause them to have trouble holding on to money and resources. Nearly a century has passed since the Great Depression impacted the world, yet the ripples of trauma from that collective experience can very much be seen today.

The second form of ancestral trauma we might encounter is intralineage trauma. These are any traumas experienced by our ancestors or past life selves that are unique to the individuals in our lineage and that were not the result of a collective event. Injuries, illnesses, unexpected deaths, abuse, personal losses, and any other events or ongoing circumstances within a family that caused trauma are considered intralineage traumas. These traumas tend to be more personal and they tend to be a bit more hidden. Most people are aware of historical global events and can somewhat imagine how collective events might have affected their ancestors, but intralineage traumas tend to be forgotten in the absence of concrete records, leaving only toxic patterns and the unconscious ancestral memory of trauma in their place.

Even the experiences our ancestors had that were intended

to be uplifting can have a significant limiting impact on a lineage and the people in it in hidden ways. Immigration, for example, is an impactful event that greatly affects the trajectory of a lineage for many generations in a very physical way and can lead to both positive change and a number of intralineage traumas. There are many reasons why people migrate from one place to another. Sometimes it is with the hope of a new start, other times it is to escape challenging and perhaps traumatic events, and other times it is by force. No matter what the circumstances are, cultural differences, language barriers, and a sense of ungroundedness that come from leaving ancestral homelands can become deeply rooted patterns that greatly impact a lineage. I have worked with many individuals who struggle to root themselves in a particular location or are often misunderstood by others despite clearly expressing themselves, all due to the energetic imprint of ancestral trauma dating back to their immigrant ancestors.

Regardless of what the ancestral trauma is, the resulting patterns manifest in a multitude of ways that are unique to each individual and each lineage. Looking at our roots and working with our Ancestral Blueprint to shine a light on these traumas begins to open many avenues for expansion and positive change. When viewed through an ancestral lens, patterns that make no sense in the context of our present-day experiences begin to make perfect sense in the context of how our ancestors lived. Understanding the root of our patterns gives us the option to heal the ways that ancestral trauma impacts our current experience, and this positive change becomes the new ripple effect felt throughout our lineage.

❧

ANCESTRAL PATTERNING

The ancestral patterns that develop through trauma are the

second form of ancestral burden that might be impacting our life experience in limiting ways. Experiences of any kind can cause an individual to repeat certain patterns and develop certain limiting beliefs and programs. These patterns can be taught as well as energetically passed down through a lineage when they are never assessed and addressed. Sometimes the experiences that create these patterns are very obviously traumatic, however other times they are simply intense, prolonged, or distinct experiences that have an impact or make an imprint in the Ancestral Blueprint.

Limiting ancestral patterns can show up in our behaviors and even our physical health. We learn how to cope with challenges and trauma from our parents through observation, direct teachings, and epigenetically. If we have an abusive father, we might observe our mother deal with the abuse by acting submissive, dissociating, or normalizing the abusive behavior. This might lead us to attract and then cope with the same treatment in similar ways in our own life because it's what we learned through observation. As a child, we might be told by our mother that we'll never find a spouse if we don't look a certain way. She was likely taught the same thing as a child, and we end up obsessing over our appearance or attracting partners that only care about looks all because of our mother's misguided teachings. Our mother may have experienced a traumatic event or elevated stress levels when she was pregnant with us, and now our nervous system has a difficult time regulating because it was exposed to elevated stress hormones while we were in the womb. We often don't have a direct choice in how we integrate ancestral patterns, yet it is still our responsibility to shift them once we recognize them.

Besides ancestral patterning that we are directly exposed to by our parents or caregivers, we may inherit older ancestral patterns that don't have an obvious origin until we dig a little deeper. Perhaps we are afraid to travel and leave our hometown.

We have never had a negative experience traveling, but every time we think about leaving we get sick to our stomach. Maybe we notice that many of our family members on our father's side have a similar distaste for leaving home too. With some investigation, we learn that the only time our grandfather left home was to fight in World War II. He came back from the war with significantly more trauma than he left with, and this personal trauma and the resulting patterns made their way into the lineage as a fear of travel.

Perhaps we were an herbalist in a past life and helped many people until our community began to persecute those they deemed to be practicing witchcraft. We learned to hide our craft and only practice in secret with those we knew were safe. Maybe the patterns created through the fear and trauma of living in this community came with us into this life, thus making us feel afraid every time we think of sharing our interest in herbalism and natural healing methods with others in the community.

The experiences of our ancestors may have been in the best interest of those who experienced them, and the patterns and beliefs they developed may have been timely or kept them safe. For us, though, these patterns are often unconscious programs that may not serve us in our current time or expression. A significant part of ancestral healing comes in the form of shifting limiting ancestral patterns that pass down through a lineage so as to not lock ourselves or future generations into these same patterns.

We can begin to explore our limiting patterns by asking ourselves what themes we notice in our own family if we are still connected to them. In what areas of life do our genetic relations have common challenges? What health imbalances seem to run in the family? Are there certain resentments or conflicts that arise consistently between members of the family? Are family members limited in certain ways when it comes to communication, money, work, education, or maintaining healthy relationships? Generational themes such as poverty, addiction, and abuse are often the result of ancestral traumas that have not been balanced. These challenging patterns can provide significant clues as to where to begin working toward healing.

Ancestral patterns can take two forms that include limiting beliefs and limiting programs. These patterns are often most noticeable as themes that we struggle with or that seem to cause friction in our lives. These themes can often be seen within a genetic lineage as patterns that repeat across the generations. If many people in a family struggle with communication, this might be a sign that there are imbalances in the ancestral patterns involving communication, for example. Ancestral religious beliefs or cultural traditions that conflict with our core truth and sense of self can also create a great amount of inner conflict for us. Additionally, ancestral trauma can lead to the development of limiting beliefs that reflect the traumatic experience, and these limiting beliefs are often passed down through lineages until the pattern is broken.

Limiting beliefs are beliefs that are not in alignment with our core truth, or our soul's true and authentic expression. We develop limiting beliefs in all sorts of ways. We form beliefs through our experiences, we have culturally taught beliefs, we also learn beliefs from our teachers, caregivers, and peers. When we think of all the ways we learn to navigate the world as children, it is easy to see how belief paradigms are passed down through a lineage by direct teaching.

Our entire reality is shaped by the lens through which we view it, and this lens is formed by our beliefs. We develop beliefs about our personal preferences, how we should act and behave, how to define our physical observations and experiences, and how the universe works. Transforming limiting beliefs into something more reflective of our truth completely changes how we experience and interact with our reality. As the lens through which we view life changes, so does what we see.

As a child, it is easy to adopt what we are told by our parents and other authority figures as truth and abandon our soul's truth. When this happens, trauma energy is created and we begin to develop limiting beliefs. Once a belief is adopted, we view our lives through the lens of this belief. Every experience we have that reflects what we have falsely learned reinforces our limiting belief. We end up making major life choices through the lens of our limiting beliefs, and our emotions and thoughts are influenced as well. If left unhealed, we may end up teaching this same belief to our children as they grow up, and the cycle continues until someone breaks it.

If we do happen to eventually heal our limiting beliefs and the trauma that created them, our life begins to take a new shape. Our thoughts and emotions become more positive and reflect a more balanced and peaceful inner landscape. We begin to make choices that reflect a new balanced truth. We also begin to manifest experiences that align with our purpose and authentic self-expression. When we swap out the metaphorical lenses of limiting beliefs for our truth, our internal and external worldview transforms into something completely new and uplifting.

Just as direct experiences and teachings can inform our beliefs, the experiences, traumas, and patterns of our ancestors can inform our beliefs as well. There are countless cases of phobias with unexplained origins that can be traced back to past life experiences or ancestral trauma. If we allow our beliefs to be informed by the fears of our ancestors, we very much limit ourselves to a life that is boxed in by walls created by long-forgotten trauma. As we observe our beliefs and mindfully work with them, we can begin to release limiting beliefs along with the traumas that formed them in the first place.

Limiting programming is the second form of ancestral pattern we can experience. These programs are formed through limiting beliefs and are an automated response to a triggering event. They contribute to unhealthy routines and habits, they cause us to unconsciously repeat the same behaviors over and over again, and they can even cause undesired autonomic responses in the body.

These limiting programs are typically created by ourselves or others as a reaction to fear and in an attempt to control our environment to promote safety. In reality, they end up limiting us and preventing us from behaving in ways that are authentic to our truth and that allow us to progress forward in positive ways. Limiting programs often keep us stuck and locked into a pattern that is very difficult to break unless it is identified and worked with in the Ancestral Blueprint.

Limiting programs often perpetuate the very things they are intended to protect us from. Perhaps when we were a child, our father left the family and we rarely ever saw him thereafter. When he did come around he would play with us and shower us with gifts, but he would always leave unexpectedly and without warning. We learned to cope with the uncertainty and loss by creating a program to protect our heart from the grief of his leaving. This program would tell us to open our heart when he was present, and to close our heart when he left.

As an adult, we might find that when we are around male father-like figures our heart is open and we can feel joy. In the absence of a father figure, our heart closes up and we have a difficult time connecting with others. This is the impact that an energetic program we create to protect ourselves from hurt and trauma can have on our well-being. A program that is meant to protect us from loss ends up depriving us of feeling love and connection in the absence of a certain type of individual.

Limiting patterns in our ancestral lineage are those that create challenge, conflict, and friction in our lives. These are the patterns that need the most attention in terms of our healing, as we often make choices through the lens of these limiting patterns that directly affect our quality and trajectory of life.

✍

LIMITING INTENTIONS

The third form of ancestral burdens we inherit are limiting intentions. Limiting intentions encompass a variety of different energetic structures and metaphysical concepts; however, the commonality among them all is that they are created out of trauma wounds, either consciously or unconsciously, and can severely limit the ability of individuals affected by them to overcome challenges and grow in positive ways. Our thoughts, emotions, and intentions have power, and if they are strong enough or consistent enough they can form energetic structures that have the possibility of influencing behavior or attracting certain circumstances. These structures can interact with our Ancestral Blueprint or our energy field in many unseen ways, and their impact can limit our sovereignty. While these limiting intentions can have a significant impact on a lineage, any of these energetic structures formed through intention can be overcome and do not necessarily affect everyone in the lineage.

One of the most influential forms of these limiting intentions are energetic contracts. Ancestral contracts are agreements that we create with other individuals in our lineage or even ourselves that cause us to act in ways that prioritize the limiting contract rather than our authentic expression. The limiting contracts we are bound by often originate from wounds within the lineage or from past life experiences we have had. We may even make contracts with ourselves that prevent us from using certain skills or accessing certain knowledge we have as a soul if our perception is that those skills or knowledge caused us pain or suffering in another lifetime. We most frequently make contracts unconsciously out of ignorance or trauma. The good news is that these ancestral contracts are often much easier to get out of than a mortgage or a business deal.

Genetic lineages often contain a variety of limiting contracts that were created prior to our incarnation into the lineage, and we are often locked into these contracts simply because we are part of the lineage. We might be the first-born son in a family, and as such, we are expected to take over the family accounting business. We might despise numbers and struggle with math, yet the expectation remains. Maybe we love helping people and really want to become a social worker, but no matter what we do, this contract's influence causes us to make decisions that go directly against our best interests and wishes. We suffer emotionally, we turn down opportunities to follow our true path in life, and we grow resentful.

We always have the power to break a contract like this once we become aware it exists, though. Our family may be upset with us and they may even try to punish us in certain ways, but when we break limiting contracts and follow our true path in life, we are always led to the resources we need to get where we are wanting to go. Once we consciously choose to break the energetic ancestral contract, we often feel a significant release and freeing of space within ourselves, and the obstacles and fears that we once perceived as impossible to overcome start to fall away on their own.

Another more nefarious-sounding limiting intention comes in the form of ancestral cursing. Cursing can seem like something right out of a fairy tale, but it begins to make sense when we look at what a curse actually is. A curse is an energetic structure that is created when a strong limiting intention has enough energy and direction behind it to manifest something. The energy required to create a curse often comes in the form of emotion or thought. With enough oomph behind it, a curse can affect any individuals that are the object of the intention as long as there is unhealed trauma, a limiting belief, or another energetic weak spot for the curse to stick to.

Now, before we start thinking of sorcerers and wizards here, curses are most often completely unconscious creations of annoyed humans. If you call to mind any time you almost had an accident because some obnoxious driver cut you off in traffic, you're on the right track. While circumstances such as these may seem inconsequential, our intentions do have an energetic impact and do manifest our physical experience, whether we are fully conscious of them or not.

A curse can amplify and attract energies and experiences that match the curse's intention, and additionally, they make it very difficult (but not impossible) to deviate from the intention of the curse. This means that whenever we experience trauma or develop patterns as a result of a harmful intention or curse, it is very difficult to overcome these patterns or traumas until the energetic structure created by the original intention is identified and replaced with our own intention.

While some curses resolve on their own through life experience, sometimes a curse and its effects get passed down from generation to generation through an entire lineage. This makes ancestral curses pretty impactful, both from the standpoint of the burden they can generate, and from the perspective of the healing that can be achieved by clearing ancestral curses.

In the case of ancestral cursing, typically individuals or groups who have experienced trauma or are living through wounded patterning act, think, and project energy in ways that are harmful or detrimental to themselves and others. Ancestral curses that are created by individuals within a lineage are often intended to protect family members or others from pain in a misguided way. Perhaps a woman marries a man who struggles to earn enough to support the family. If she thinks about it enough, feels strongly enough, and perhaps has an intention that her children will never make the same mistake she did, an ancestral curse can be created that causes future generations of women in the lineage to sacrifice their happiness in a relationship for money or security.

It may seem far-fetched to think that a strong intention backed by grief and anger from a person we have never known that lived hundreds or even thousands of years ago could have a significant impact on our life now. If we consider that our intentions shape how we act, react, and navigate life, though, we can begin to see how the influence of a harmful intention from long ago can grow like cancer in a lineage.

Besides curses and contracts, there are a variety of other energetic structures that can be formed through intention and affect us personally or influence our Ancestral Blueprint. It may seem like a daunting task to uncover and address all of the influences of limiting intentions that could possibly be affecting us from generations past. It's important to remember, though, that regardless of the terminology we use to identify and catego-rize these energetic structures, they are all simply creations made through intention. If intention created it, intention can change it or eliminate it altogether, and it is with intention that we will begin unearthing and healing our ancestral burdens.

While it may seem unfair that our lives to some degree reflect the presence of our ancestors' trauma energies, unhealthy patterns, and the limiting intentions influencing them, we must remember that we were not born into a vacuum. Our ability to be alive on Earth at this time is only possible because there is a lineage of people behind us that paved the way for our entry into this life. Our bodies, our unique DNA, and every part of us that make us a physical being only exist because of the intentions and experiences of our ancestors. Life does not discriminate. We inherit the good and the bad, the uplifting and the challenging, the strengths and weaknesses. Often our soul grows the most from healing the imbalances passed down to us through our lineage. While we may get frustrated at times, especially when things become difficult, there is a purpose and growth to come from doing this work.

It's usually in hindsight that we are able to see the deeper purpose and meaning of our past experiences. When my life took a detour and I found myself suddenly grappling with my own ancestral and personal trauma healing process, I had already been working with energy and teaching spiritual and metaphysical healing practices for years. Still, I was not impervious to the pain, suffering, and general challenges that come with healing. No matter who we are or how advanced our spiritual or healing knowledge is, we still deeply feel unresolved energies from our past as they leave. This is how we learn, understand, and grow as humans, and it is an essential but difficult part of healing and spiritual transformation work.

In the midst of releasing the painful trauma from my past, I found it very difficult to see the positive meaning and purpose of my experiences. Through this intensive healing process, all I could see were my losses and everything I had to give up to overcome my past. I severed all of my familial connections permanently and became an orphan overnight. I lost all of my personal connections when I realized that they were a reflection of the unremembered and unhealed trauma that I carried from my past and my lineage. I could no longer give them what they wanted to take from me, and so they either fell away or I cut them off myself. My clients went elsewhere when I had to take time for my own healing and trauma recovery, and so my successful and deeply loved business faded into the ethers until I was able to rebirth it in a new form. Most of all, I lost myself, or at least the self I thought I was for most of my life.

These losses were the greatest blessings I have ever received in my life, but it took the emergence from my cocoon of healing to fully see this perspective. As I grieved the loss of my false life and the potential I saw for that life that I finally understood could never have been realized, I invited in the new.

After my healing process, I slowly but surely received all of the people, experiences, joys, physical healing, connections, and gifts that I had envisioned and prayed for in my past. I could never have manifested these very balanced and beautiful facets of my life through the abusive people or limiting circumstances that existed in my life prior to my dark-night healing journey. I finally realized that the techniques I used to heal myself that were gifted to me by Spirit were not a long shot or a hope or a fantasy. I did the work and the very fabric of my life and my being transformed rapidly and completely.

The faster I let go and healed the imbalances in my Ancestral Blueprint, the more quickly my life changed for the better, even if I couldn't feel it at the time. I was guided, held, given the resources and support, and uplifted each day until I was ready to reemerge into the world as a new, more aligned version of myself. Healing deeply on an energetic and ancestral level was no longer a theoretical avenue of transformation for me. It became a very real and lived truth through my own experience of it, and it became my mission to share what I learned with those I would connect with moving forward.

The beauty of life is that we have the ability to change, adapt, and grow. We are not stuck with the hand we are dealt or choose. Our ancestral burdens are something we can learn from and balance. It is choosing not to heal or being unaware that the choice to heal exists that has contributed to the perpetuation of ancestral burdens throughout lineages worldwide. The more we choose the path of healing and the path of responsibility for what exists inside our Ancestral Blueprint, the more balanced our lives become and the more we are able to rise above the limitations that our ancestors could not overcome.

Ultimately, healing our ancestral burdens is about freeing

ourselves and claiming sovereignty over our experience of life. We never incarnate into a lineage that does not serve our growth in some way, and we are never given an experience that we do not have the skills and soul knowledge to overcome. Ancestral burdens are nothing more than imbalances that need balancing to live our most authentic, sovereign, and blissful life.

Chapter 3

The Healing Path

Before we start tinkering with our Ancestral Blueprint, it's helpful to have a basic understanding of how healing works in the first place. No matter where our personal healing journey ends up taking us, having a map, some supplies, and a team of very skilled allies are essential. They keep us from getting lost and greatly accelerate our journey. Unfortunately, in many cases no one has bothered to tell us about these available tools and support, and figuring this out on our own can take anywhere from decades to lifetimes. The good news is, we all have these things available to us if we just know where to look.

We often struggle so much to overcome our traumas and limiting patterns because the ancestral wisdom of how to heal and the practices and social structures meant to help us do that have been lost to us. The only way to reclaim this wisdom that is inherently ours is to tap into the threads of ancestral knowledge that still exist within us or have someone who has already reintegrated this lost wisdom awaken the seeds of that knowledge.

Regardless of how we come to remember what we already

know, truth can always be felt in our hearts, our blood, and our bones. When we encounter the energy or frequency of truth outside of ourselves, it awakens the frequency of truth in our own bodies and in our Ancestral Blueprint. This is the frequency and subsequent understanding that is meant to be awakened here so that your internal knowing and your ancestral wisdom within can be ignited through the words on these pages. With this in mind, we proceed with the map of our healing journey.

❧

PREREQUISITES FOR HEALING

In order to fully heal or transform anything at all, five prerequisites must be met. These prerequisites together form a healing framework I developed based on the intuitive guidance I was given through my healing process that I call The ROESA Method™. These prerequisites can be met in an infinite number of ways through an infinite number of practices. No matter what form they take, though, once these prerequisites are met, healing and transformation commence. We often struggle to overcome our limitations because we are not aware of these prerequisites. The healing itself is quite simple, but gaining the complete understanding we need in order to allow for healing is where we get hung up.

To begin this process, we first need to ask ourselves, "What is *real*?" This is the "R" in ROESA. Exploring what is real or what exists as part of our reality ignites a journey of self-discovery and transformation. It may seem obvious, but becoming aware of what exists in our personal experience that is limiting for us is often not as simple as it may seem. If we are diligent and constantly observing, we may notice most of the weeds that pop up in our garden, but there are always those that hide under other plants or remain unseen until they grow large enough to cause trouble. Many of the limiting or toxic dynamics operating in our lives and our lineage live in the realm of shadow and the unconscious. This means that until we become aware that certain patterns, influences, intentions, circumstances, traumas, connections, emotions, or energies exist, it is difficult or impossible to work with them in a meaningful way.

I spent years doing my inner work and healing in the best ways I could prior to my unexpected trauma healing experience. I always believed that to be the best healer and teacher I could be, I needed to practice what I preached. Years of inner work improved chronic illness, autoimmune disease, the quality of my relationships to a degree, and my work life, but unexplained challenges and the questionable motives of people in my life remained an unsolved mystery. I had a difficult time understanding why certain patterns kept repeating in my life even though I was "doing the work" so to speak, but I persisted with my commitment to healing nonetheless.

I have always been deeply committed to my personal spiritual and healing work throughout my adult life, but I didn't fully know what was "real" for me until I began remembering and viscerally re-experiencing PTSD flashbacks of childhood abuse in my late thirties. The hidden traumas and locked-away experiences of my past had an extremely significant energetic and physical impact on my external life circumstances and inner landscape my entire life. Until I remembered what had happened to me, though, there was very little I could do to fully heal those experiences and their impact.

My life and relationships were manifested reflections of my childhood trauma even though I didn't remember over a decade of abuse until twenty-five years after it ended. The energies and impact of my personal and ancestral traumas were there, though, waiting to be discovered at exactly the right time.

Sometimes what is very real and has a very tremendous impact on us takes some digging into the hidden recesses of our consciousness, or in my case the serendipitous timing of Spirit, to reveal. It's never our fault that we can't see what is hidden, but it is our job to keep our eyes open and not turn a blind eye when we do finally see the darker parts of our experience that need attention.

Healing takes a significant amount of mindfulness and self-awareness. The ability to step back and take a look at our feelings, actions, beliefs, and challenges from the perspective of the neutral observer is a critical skill to develop for anyone on a path of personal growth and healing. Observing what exists is an act of bringing the unconscious aspects of our being into our conscious awareness. It is an act of shining light on what lies hidden in the darkness. We cannot heal what we cannot see, so seeing is the first step on this journey.

The second step of the ROESA Method is to trace what we have become aware of, to whatever capacity is possible, back to its roots. We ask ourselves, "What is the *origin*?" Understanding the events and intentions that created the imbalances we would like to heal in the first place begins the process of learning and growth. When we understand how something came to be, we can fully see what exists in its wholeness - from its inception to its current state. This step is crucial, for it allows us to work with the entire energetic expression of an imbalance.

Even very personal traumas, such as those I experienced in childhood, often do not originate from our current lifetime. I was not the first in my genetic lineage to experience the types of sexual, emotional, and psychological abuse that I endured. The beliefs, programming, and traumas that allowed for such darkness to persist and express in my lineage had roots long ago with people from a different time and place altogether. I was born into an ancestral story that began long before I incarnated into my genetic lineage. Everything is connected, and as extreme as my experience was, the origin of my traumas and their impact on my life predated my own lifetime by many generations and were influenced by many factors beyond the relationship between myself and my abusers. It is in addressing these factors that extend beyond the scope of our personal experience that we dive into the realms of ancestral healing, and this is where the real work and the progress happen.

If we think of an imbalance as a weed in our garden, it is impossible to permanently remove the weed if we just pull off the flowers or the stem. We need to pull it out by its roots to fully address it. This is what we are doing when we trace the origin of an imbalance. Finding the root of an imbalance does not mean we need to dwell on the past or ruminate on our traumas either. It simply means that we look at the entire picture, see it in its entirety, and move on to our next steps.

This brings us to the third prerequisite for healing, which is to understand how the things we can now see in their whole expression are impacting us in unbalanced or limiting ways and have influenced our experience. For this step, we ask, "What is the *effect?*" This is the step of seeing how the weed is impacting our garden. Is it choking out the other plants? Is it using up all the nutrients in the soil? Is it attracting pests?

When we finally see the weeds and how they are destroying what we are trying to create, it is very difficult to ignore them. Seeing the impact of our past and how our ancestral wounds and generational trauma prevent us from accessing the life that we most desire not only gives us a clearer picture of what we need to change, but it also allows us to determine how we want to change things.

Understanding gives us the power to make a decision about how we want to change what we see, and this act of conscious choice to change is the fourth step in the ROESA Method. We must ask ourselves, "How do I want this to *shift?*" If we can't envision a shift in our experience, change can't happen. We may know what exists, where it came from, and how it impacts us, but we are stuck with our imbalances until we decide how we want things to change.

Once we have addressed the first four steps of this healing framework, we now have to take action toward making the changes that we've decided upon. This action comes in the form of giving permission to our body, higher self, higher power, or all of the above to release the energies that are not in alignment with the changes we desire. From here, healing immediately commences. In this step, we *authorize* the change.

A significant aspect of healing involves conscious awareness. When we become consciously aware of what exists, why it exists, and how it influences us, we have the power of choice. Choice gives us the opportunity to work with what we become consciously aware of in a new way, and to transform everything that exists in our experience into something that supports balance, positive growth, love, and upliftment. This is alchemy.

This transformation process can take an infinite number of forms. There are countless healing modalities, rituals, and therapeutic practices from many traditions that are effective as healing tools. Additionally, the experiences we have in life are often our greatest teachers, and our experiences and the choices we make through our experiences are enough to create significant healing and positive growth when we meet these prerequisites. Regardless of the shape it takes or the lens through which it is viewed, the reason any healing works is because an awareness and conscious understanding of an imbalance has been reached, a choice to change has been made, and permission has been given to release the imbalance and to anchor the new balanced expression into our being.

The degree to which this process works is dependent upon the degree to which conscious understanding has been reached by a person needing healing, as well as the degree to which all parts of themselves - conscious and unconscious, higher and lower - are on board with the changes that need to be made to shift an imbalance. This means healing can be an extremely simple process for some things, and it can be a multi-layered and nuanced process for others. Either way, the more we work toward self-awareness and choose to prioritize healing and the transformation of imbalances in all aspects of our lives, the more fruitful and transformative the healing process will be.

In the case of ancestral healing, finding the root cause of an imbalance may seem like an impossible task, especially when the origin of an imbalance could be from a past life we have no memory of or a genetic ancestor from twelve generations back in our lineage. Healing therapies that only address the physical or the mind often fall short when it comes to healing an imbalance because it is so difficult to truly access the origin of an imbalance when that information lies beyond the physical. There is much more to us as people and more to life than just our mind and our physical experiences. If we truly want to heal all aspects of ourselves, we have to incorporate all aspects of our being into the healing, and this includes what lies beyond the physical and the mental.

❧
YOUR SPIRITUAL SUPPORT TEAM

It is the spiritual connections and aspects of our being that often hold the most wisdom. It is these spiritual connections and understandings that our ancestors from long ago, whomever they may have been, relied upon to guide them and bring balance to their lives. For us as the self-selected healers of our lineage, this is where our spiritual support team, intuition, and a whole lot of trust and faith come in.

Our Ancestral Blueprint contains all of the information we need to transform any imbalances in our lineage, but even with a finely-tuned intuition, it can be very difficult to see the forest through the trees. Our guides, higher self, and Spirit can see the whole picture though, and working with our spiritual support team is a necessity if we want to make this journey of ancestral healing easier and more complete. Without this spiritual support, we may get caught up in our blind spots or lack the energy or intuitive sight needed to identify the unbalanced energies that are limiting our lives.

Luckily, the limitations we experience as humans are not limitations that Spirit experiences. Spirit can move mountains for us as long as we know the mountain is there, know where it came from, understand how it affects us, know where we want to move it, and give Spirit permission to move it for us. Our spiritual support team will always come through for us, as long as what we are asking of them is in our highest good and the highest good of all.

This brings up another important concept in healing. Healing is never really healing unless it is done for the highest good of all. This means that any imbalances we would like to transform for ourselves and our lineage cannot be completely brought into balance unless the healing benefits all. If an effort to balance an imbalance is not done with the alignment of being of benefit to all, more imbalance can be created unintentionally.

As humans, it is impossible for us to know every detail of how the changes we desire will impact others and ourselves in the future. This is why working with our spiritual support team is so critical for healing, as they will never take an action that could potentially harm ourselves or others. They are our safety net, and they ensure that when we embark on a healing journey that the journey is actually healing and leads to positive growth.

Intuitive communication with my spirit guides is something I have developed over the course of many years. It is this relationship that I attribute to saving my life on countless occasions, helping me overcome the most treacherous of experiences, and teaching me highly effective spiritual and healing concepts in a balanced and truthful manner. If it was not for my spiritual support team, I would not be here to share these words and methods with you, and for that, I am eternally grateful. No matter how challenging things become I know that my guides are always there as a beacon for my heart to follow, even if my mind can't see it.

We have many different guides and spiritual beings that support us and guide us throughout our life. Different traditions have different names and terminology for these beings, so feel free to use whatever terminology fits into your understanding and spiritual tradition. This higher power for you might be your own "big" self - or what I call the higher self. This is the part of you that transcends your human ego. You may also call upon supportive and balanced beings such as a guardian angel, deities from different ancestral or spiritual traditions, galactic beings, ascended masters such as Jesus or Gautama Buddha, or a group of these beings. I refer to them as guides in these pages, but follow your own tradition and understanding. You may also call upon whatever you consider to be the highest power of all. You can refer to this power as God, Source, Great Mother, Creator, Spirit, love, quantum particles, or anything else that fits into your understanding.

The most important thing with regard to healing is to always call upon your higher power for support and to give that higher power permission to work with you. Permission is key, as Spirit will never take action without permission from either your conscious human self or your higher self, and the wishes of your higher self will always supersede the wishes of your human self.

When we begin doing ancestral work, it is often helpful to call upon the support of ancestral guides. While we have many different guides that have experience, wisdom, and skills to offer us, our ancestral guides are unique in that they deeply understand the human experience and are directly connected to us through our Ancestral Blueprint. This means that our ancestral guides are also invested in our healing and personal development in a unique way because any healing we do impacts and benefits our entire lineage, including them.

Ancestral guides serve as keepers of their lineage and cultivators of healed ancestral energies. They may also work with many individuals within the lineage that they come from, as they deeply understand the themes and patterns that have been passed down through the lineage and have unique wisdom to share for working through these dynamics.

Our ancestral guides can originate from either our soul lineage or our genetic lineage, and in some cases are connected to both, as there can be some crossover between these two aspects of our Ancestral Blueprint. These guides can originate from any point in linear time in our genetic lineage's past or soul's existence, from our current generation back to many thousands of lifetimes ago or even into our linear future. They often have a very good understanding of the skills and wisdom that we personally bring into the lineage that is of benefit. This means that they can work with us to help us activate and share our unique gifts with our lineage to facilitate healing and balance.

Ancestors that we might connect with and ancestral guides are not necessarily the same thing, and there are distinct differences between an ancestor and an ancestral guide. We may have unhealed ancestors that we connect with as we work through our healing who can be equally as wounded or lacking in understanding as a living human. These ancestors may have their own agenda that does not necessarily benefit the entire lineage. In some cases they may demand that we take certain actions, exhibit lower emotions such as fear or anger, or need help and guidance themselves. This means that we must be mindful when connecting with any of our ancestors, practice healthy discernment, and never assume that all ancestors are guides.

In contrast, our ancestral guides unconditionally love us and also understand that our growth will benefit the entire lineage. Ancestral guides are always healed ancestors who have mastered and balanced the majority of the ancestral burdens created through their incarnations and have chosen to serve as a guide rather than incarnating again. They will never appear angry, fearful, or disappointed in us, and they never blame us or judge our actions or behavior. Our guides will never place conditions on their guidance or connection with us, and they will never violate our free will or tell us what to do.

Guides will work with us consciously if we choose; however, they will not connect with us in a conscious way unless we initiate that form of contact or choose to work with them directly. If we do not initiate direct contact or conscious relationship with our guides, they will communicate and guide through inspiration, synchronicity, and opportunity. Regardless of how we choose to connect with our guides, they are always guiding us and directing us toward information and experiences that will teach us and help us grow.

As you begin your ancestral healing journey, it is quite helpful to start cultivating a relationship with your guides if you have not done so already. If you choose to take this step, know that your guides will never do harm, they will never do something you are not ready for, and they will never lie to you (although they won't be held accountable for how you interpret their messages). If you are ready to take the first step toward consciously partnering with your guides for your healing, recite the following statement out loud or in your mind:

I call upon my ancestral guides, spirit guides, higher self, and Spirit to surround me with their love, support, healing, and wisdom. On this day, by my own free will choice, I give permission for my guides and Spirit to work with me in a direct and conscious way that serves my highest good and the highest good of all creation. I give permission to be guided and to receive healing that honors my genetic and soul lineages, my purpose and highest path in life, and the evolution of my unique Ancestral Blueprint into its most balanced state. I give permission to receive healing that will remove blocks and limitations that would prevent me from connecting with my guides, higher self, and Spirit more deeply. Thank you guides, thank you higher self, and thank you Spirit for your eternal and unconditionally loving support.

Once you have spoken this statement, you will find that when you are truly ready, your guides will begin gradually connecting with you in ways that are more concrete. There are many ways that our guides communicate with us, and how this communication comes through is typically the path of least resistance. If you are a person who notices synchronicities such as repeating numbers, messages on license plates, seeing specific animals, running across feathers, and so forth, this may be how your guides first begin communicating with you. If you are quick to pick up on thoughts or ideas, they may give you downloads of information, vivid dreams, or ideas that just pop into your mind at the perfect time. If you have a developed intuition, they will likely communicate with you intuitively in a way that is most easeful for you.

Our relationship with our guides and how we consciously work with them can and usually will transform over time. As we heal and become more attuned, it becomes easier for us to receive the messages that we need from our guides in different ways. When I first began working with my guides consciously, they primarily communicated with me using synchronicity and by guiding me to information that I needed. If I asked for a question to be answered, I would then come across a book that contained the answer somewhere in its pages, pull an oracle card that guided me in the right direction, or see a license plate with an important word on it.

As I continued to cultivate this relationship, I began noticing other signals that they would give me. I would hear a high-pitched ringing in my ear if a certain group of guides were wanting to connect. Other guides would make a spot on the back of my head vibrate if they had a message for me. Many years into doing this work, I can now see my guides clairvoyantly, hear my guides' words clairaudiently, and I am an active channel for my guides in written and spoken format. Despite this conscious relationship I have developed with my guides, they still regularly send me license plates to get my attention when I'm out and about living my life.

There really is no right or wrong way to connect with our guides and Spirit in general. The most important thing is that we are open to their support and actively work to engage with our guides as spiritual support and our partners in healing. Asking our guides questions, requesting healing from them, and giving them permission to support us are all important aspects of our side of this beautiful relationship. Mindfully paying attention to messages we receive, regardless of the format, and acting on their guidance will strengthen this relationship each day.

One helpful exercise that can open more active communication with spirit guides is a practice called automatic writing. When first trying this exercise, it is best to begin with a topic that you are not particularly emotionally invested in. This helps the ego step aside and your guides step forward when you first begin. Over time, as you practice this form of communication it will become easier to discern your ego from your guides' answers.

Begin this practice by writing a question at the top of a piece of paper. Take a few deep breaths and relax. Invite your guides to connect with you and communicate through you. Then allow one word at a time to enter your mind. Write each word as it comes into your mind without thinking about what the words are going to be. Keep writing one word at a time as they enter your mind until you feel as if the message is complete. Then go back and read what you have written. Did it answer your question? Did it bring insight? Was it helpful? Try this exercise any time you are needing support or guidance from your spirit guides. The more you practice, the more insight you will gain, and the better you will get at this form of communication.

One of the most important functions of our guides with regard to ancestral healing besides their guidance, is the healing and clearing of energy they can provide for us. You do not have to be trained as an energy healer yourself or pay for a healer to work with you to receive healing. Your guides can do much of the heavy lifting for you when you give them permission and demonstrate that you have met the prerequisites for healing the specific issue you are working on. This means that you can ask your guides to do healing for you whenever you want to, and they will do whatever they can for you that is in your highest good. The more specific you can be with your requests and the more you can demonstrate your understanding and awareness of the issue, the more they can do for you.

Healers and other trained individuals can share their insight, knowledge from their experience, intuitive information they receive, and their skills as a healer, and they can offer much-needed human support and loving care as well. Nevertheless, you are always capable of acting as your own healer without any special skills as long as you are committed to your healing path and are willing to employ your guides as your personal healing team.

❧
THE IMPACT OF RELEASE

It is important to know that through this process of ancestral healing you will be clearing energy. When we clear energy, there are many ways that we can experience it, some of which are very physical. Each person clears energy in a unique way, and each imbalance has a unique way of leaving the body. Common clearing symptoms include tingling sensations in the body, hot or cold sensations, yawning, burping, tremoring of the muscles, dizziness, emotional release, aching or pain in areas of the body, and tiredness. You may experience any number of these things when healing occurs. It is important to be aware of clearing symptoms and to allow the body to release in whatever ways it is wanting or needing to. The more healing work you do, the more you will become familiar with how your body processes and releases energy. With practice and experience, you will learn your limits and you will learn how to help your body release more quickly.

Any time we release trauma energy or dense emotional energy, there are a few things we can experience that can feel challenging. Our physical body is a sensory device that is capable of translating energy into something we can under-stand. This means that our physical body reacts to the energies it experiences, regardless of whether those energies are coming or going. When we release old repressed emotional energy, we often feel these emotions or even anxiety as they are released. When we release trauma energy, our nervous system and body can react as if there is a threat as the energy leaves, which can then put us into a temporary state of dysregulation. When we release limiting beliefs, patterns, and programs from the past, we can often have thoughts or memories from the past pop into our mind as these energies clear. What goes in must come out, and we often experience it in some way as it leaves.

Experiencing any of these things, especially if we have repressed and avoided feeling them for years, can be alarming if we don't understand what is happening. This is why it's important to go into healing armed with this knowledge and to be prepared for what we might feel during and up to several days after energy healing work. It is also important to have the physical support of the human connections that we have as we release these energies, as this can help us process what is released and provide us with the emotional support that we might need. Once energies from the past clear from our being, we are left feeling much lighter and we no longer experience the effects of these energies in our physical lives and internal landscape.

After completing any healing, it is important to follow a self-care routine to help balance and ground your energy. Drinking plenty of water is essential, as energy release can be dehydrating and water helps us flush both physical and energetic toxins from our bodies. A walk in nature and a salt bath or shower can be extremely beneficial after healing to help clear any remaining dense energies that are ready to leave your body. Allow yourself to rest or nap if you feel a bit off after a healing and ask your guides to help you clear any energies that are ready to leave while you sleep. It can also be helpful to record any information or experiences you have in a journal, and talking through any insights you might gain through your healing with a friend, family member, healer, coach, or counselor can be very beneficial as well. Most of all, live your life, be kind to yourself, love yourself, don't judge yourself, and work through the forthcoming exercises only when you feel guided to and at a pace that feels manageable.

Now that we have opened ourselves to a deeper connection with our guides and are aware of the prerequisites for the most complete healing to occur, we are ready to begin actively working with our Ancestral Blueprint.

Part 2

Techniques for Healing
Ancestral Burdens

Chapter 4

Healing Ancestral Trauma

Trauma is an interesting concept because it has so many varied definitions depending on the model used to approach it. The medical model defines it differently than the psychotherapeutic model, and even within psychotherapy practices there are many different definitions of trauma. As an energy healer, my experience with trauma is as an energy that informs our physical experience, and so I use and define the word trauma here through that lens.

Trauma energy is created whenever we have an experience that causes us to use that experience to inform our thoughts, emotions, beliefs, and choices rather than our authentic core truth. Any time we have an experience that is painful, causes us to feel fear, or creates suffering, there is a possibility that parts of us will begin to adopt a new perception of reality based on the experience rather than maintain our core truth, or the love-based truth of our soul. When we reject our core truth in exchange for fear and separation, a fracturing occurs within us and we develop different parts or aspects of ourselves that operate through the lens of the fracturing experience. Trauma energy is created whenever this internal fracturing occurs, and this trauma energy and its effects inform our physical, mental, emotional, and spiritual experience until the inner fracturing is repaired through the inner work of reclaiming our core truth. It is this internal fracturing that indicates that an experience has become a trauma for a person.

When looking at the impact of a traumatic experience on a person, it is nearly impossible to judge how an event will affect them based on the type of experience alone. Any experience at all can create internal fracturing and trauma energy, from a single sentence spoken by a caregiver to living through a war. Our personal opinions about how an event should or should not impact someone is certainly not to be used as an indicator of the true impact that experience has actually had on a person.

From an energetic perspective, the ways that trauma can impact a person are primarily based on how much an experience has caused them to fall out of alignment with their core truth, or how much internal fracturing has occurred. The more fracturing there is, the more severe the effect of the trauma will be. This is why complex trauma can be so much more challenging to identify and heal than trauma from a single event. With repeated experiences that create fear, pain, and massive shifts in one's truth based on those experiences, many layers of fracturing are created within the self that must be addressed and repaired in order to heal.

This same concept can be applied to a lineage as well, as the events and experiences that cause us to fall out of alignment with our truth are not limited to this one lifetime or even our own personal experiences. Centuries of ancestral trauma can be passed down to us through our lineage and anchored into our experience by our Ancestral Blueprint. This ancestral trauma inheritance can be activated by a single event that reflects a theme similar to the original trauma. Once ancestral trauma energy is activated within us and we begin having experiences reflective of our inherited ancestral trauma, this trauma becomes our responsibility and a burden we share with our ancestors. Ancestral trauma is big and it continues to grow and cause damage in its wake until someone in the lineage decides to mend the fractures within themselves rather than allow them to perpetuate.

When we begin the work of digging up our roots to see what lies beneath the surface, we often find that of all the weeds in our garden, the vast majority are seeded from trauma. There is a very good reason for this, for trauma itself is the most dense energy we can hold in our being. Trauma energy acts as a massive weighty magnet carrying the imprint of the original trauma. It both anchors us down into and magnetizes to us challenging and fear-based life experiences that are in resonance with the themes of the original trauma. The longer trauma energy is left unresolved, the more it replicates itself in our lives in a variety of ways.

The story doesn't end here, though. Trauma energy also acts like a web that holds repressed emotions, limiting beliefs, limiting intentions, and all other energies created as a result of the original trauma into our being. This means that until the original trauma energy is cleared, everything that is held in place by this trauma net will be left unresolved to some degree and the web will hold more and more energy as the trauma replicates itself through subsequent life experiences.

As one might imagine, this can make for a massive energetic burden, and it is often a burden that is very difficult or impossible for a single individual to carry alone. When the weight becomes too much and an individual is not able to balance the trauma, the burden is often energetically shared with an individual's connections - sometimes by choice and sometimes by force - and here we have the beginnings of ancestral trauma weaving its way through a lineage. Unhealed trauma energy acts like a cancer not only in the lives of individuals who have experienced it, but it grows and spreads through soul and genetic lineages as well.

When we consider how significant the impact of trauma can be for an individual and a lineage, it begins to feel impossible to work through every little ancestral trauma that exists in the Ancestral Blueprint of a person. The good news is that once we are able to identify the original trauma to some degree and its impact, we can clear a large majority of the energies that exist inside of the trauma net. When we remove the imprint and energy of trauma, there is nothing left to hold the limiting patterns and energies created through the trauma in place. Just as trauma can be the most limiting of all influences on a person and lineage, it can also be the most liberating to heal.

From an energetic perspective, healing anything at all involves restoring balance to all aspects of whatever needs healing, starting with the energetic components. Everything physical that exists or that we experience begins as energy and essentially is energy, so it is impossible to restore balance to our physical experience if the energetic components that contribute to a condition are not balanced first.

The healing process for ancestral trauma always requires that the prerequisites for healing be met at some level. How deep we have to go to pull out our ancestral trauma by its roots is largely influenced by how much that trauma is impacting our current life experience and whether or not there is soul growth we can achieve by digging a little deeper. No matter what our path of ancestral trauma healing is, it will be unique, it will be layered, it may be challenging, and it will have an unimaginable positive impact.

GENETIC LINEAGE TRAUMA HEALING

The easiest way to begin the ancestral trauma healing process is to address the burdens we are carrying that are not ours to carry. While we have many of our own traumas and patterns that will need to be addressed through our healing process, we may also be holding a multitude of energies from many generations back in our genetic lineage that have been passed down to us through our Ancestral Blueprint that do not belong to us. We often aren't aware that we are toting around our ancestors' energies with us, but we are impacted by these energies nonetheless.

Ancestral trauma energies that were passed down to us, but never belonged to us, can create several harmful outcomes. At the very least we could be prolonging our ancestors' suffering because we are holding the energies that could help them identify and heal their traumas. This limits their ability to grow in the ways their soul desires. At the very worst, we might be teaching them that they can simply unload their trauma energies into us or another person any time they feel uncomfortable and we give them a reason to avoid healing altogether. Additionally, these ancestral trauma energies are capable of activating similar themes in our own lives to our detriment, causing us to have to work through our own trauma that has been created in the wake of these ancestral energies that never belonged to us in the first place.

It is very important to understand that we can never heal internal fracturing in someone else by taking on or holding their challenging energies for them. We all learn and grow through our challenges and are responsible for addressing and balancing the energies created within us ourselves. A person's ability to grow through challenging experiences is limited when we hold their energies in our energy field for them. If we are holding burdensome energies that belong to others, we prevent them from working through their limitations and traumas themselves.

We are each responsible for our own energies, so we really can't heal someone else's trauma for them even if we want to.

This is why ancestral trauma energies and patterns that have been passed down through lineages are so pervasive. We often don't know that some of what we are carrying doesn't belong to us, and we don't understand that it's also impossible for us to heal these foreign energies and patterns. If we can't heal what has been passed down to us, we often just keep holding, repressing, and manifesting through these energies, which opens the path for these patterns to continue working their way into future generations. With this in mind, it is best to identify what we are holding that doesn't belong to us so that we can release responsibilities that aren't ours.

So, what do we do with the things we are holding that don't belong to us? We give them back. Returning energies that do not belong to us to their origin can allow us to release a significant portion of the ancestral burden we are holding without diving too deeply into the nature of these energies. This process also allows actual healing to occur, as opposed to the pattern of holding, repressing, and passing down these energies to future generations.

Let's begin this work by imagining that our entire being - the physical, mental, emotional, energetic, and spiritual aspects - is a house. Picture this beautiful house in your mind. It is full of all kinds of things. Some of these things might be very useful, some might be gathering dust in a corner, some might be broken and need repair, and others might be a hindrance in some way. Many of these items you have bought yourself, some have been given to you as gifts, and others are part of an inheritance that has been passed down to you. These items represent the energies and patterns that belong to you and are your responsibility to work through and heal.

Now imagine that there is a basement in your house. This basement is full of objects that don't belong to you, and you may have no idea where they came from. These items belong to other people in your genetic lineage, and they take up space in your house rent-free. Picture this basement in your mind, and notice how much space these objects take up. Are there just a few? Is it packed floor-to-ceiling? Make note of how much of your basement is being used by others in your lineage to store energies that have no business being in your house. To get this basement cleaned out, we have to figure out where all of this stuff came from and we're going to need some help.

First, we're going to need some tools and support to work through this healing process. Gather together a pen, notecards or scraps of paper, and a basket or container and arrange them in front of you. Next, you will need to call in your spiritual support team. You may use the following phrase or create your own using your terminology:

I call in my guides, higher self, and Spirit and ask that they create sacred space around me for this healing. I give permission now for assistance and guidance in releasing the ancestral energies I am holding in my being that do not belong to me and in returning them to their rightful place. I ask that this healing be performed for my highest good and the highest good of all creation. Thank you for your support, your wisdom, and your healing.

Next, we begin the process of returning the ancestral burdens that are not ours to carry to their rightful owner. Following your inner guidance, choose a side of your genetic family to begin with, either your biological mother's lineage or your biological father's. We will stick with one individual in your genetic lineage for now and repeat this process for others at a later time.

When you have chosen a side of your genetic ancestral lineage to work with, grab your notecards and write your biological mother or father's name, or simply "mother" or "father" if you do not know their name, on the card. Place the card several feet in front of you and position your basket or container between yourself and this card. Now place your hands over the basket and intend that it be filled with all of the energies that belong to your parent that are not yours to carry. Ask your guides or Spirit to assist you in this process. You may use the following phrase or create your own:

Guides, please assist me in filling this basket with any ancestral energies, including emotions, trauma, and other burdens, that belong to my (ancestor's name or title here) and are in my highest good to release from my being now.

Your guides will instantly begin to help you transport all of the relevant energies into this basket. Take a moment to close your eyes and visualize your basket in front of you full of your ancestor's energy. Is the basket full? Does it look heavy? What color or shape does this energy take?

Next, ask your guides to show you what this burden feels like in your body. Notice any pressure, pain, or emotion that rises to the surface. The image you see in your mind that represents this individual's energy in the basket and the sensations or emotions you feel in your body should give you a sense of how this energy is impacting you.

In this next step, we will begin the process of returning the energies that do not belong to us to their rightful place. It does not matter whether you have been or are still physically connected to your ancestor in this life. Your intention is enough to complete this process. Imagine that the notecard you have written on represents the individual in your lineage you are working with. Lift the basket in front of you and place it on the notecard, then repeat the following:

The energies in this basket belong to you and they are your responsibility. I am sorry that you experienced this trauma,

78

but I cannot heal it for you and I am not willing to continue to hold it, as it is harming me and the future generations that it may be passed down to through me. I am returning this energy to you now and I give permission for my guides, higher self, and Spirit to remove these foreign energies and the energetic connections and structures that allowed them to come into my being, and return them to their rightful place in a manner that serves the highest good of all.

As you give permission to return these energies to your family member, you may feel sensations or react to the release of these energies from your body. Trust whatever you are experiencing and know that you will never experience something that is too much for you. Once the energies have been passed back, it is important to offer assistance with releasing the burden that these energies represent for your ancestor. You can do this by stating the following to your ancestor as if they are standing in front of you:

I now request that healing be performed by Spirit to release this trauma from you should you be willing to accept this healing.

Once you have requested healing, trust that they have either accepted or rejected healing, regardless of whether or not you are able to receive their answer yourself. By offering healing, you are giving your ancestor an opportunity to heal. With this step complete you have done your job and met your responsibility to these energies.

It is not necessary to take any physical action beyond the offering of healing. If the individual you are working with is not ready to receive healing for their trauma, this is absolutely okay. Not everyone will be ready to do the work required to overcome their trauma, or the timing may not be right for them to do this work. This is why we turn things over to Spirit to manage, as we can never fully know what is best for someone else.

If your ancestor accepts healing for the trauma energies that have been passed back, Spirit will release and recycle the energies that they are ready to release, and will provide them with the opportunities needed to heal whatever remains. If your ancestor is not ready to heal, Spirit will return the energy to them or hold it for them until the time is right to heal. Either way, the burden is released from you.

Once this process is complete for the biological parent you have chosen to work with, you can now go back and repeat this same process for other ancestors and generations of your lineage. You can choose to work with one line of your genetic lineage at a time, or you can work with one generation at a time. The choice is yours, so follow your inner knowing as to how you would like to proceed.

As you work backward through your lineage with this release process, you will begin by passing back energies to each individual one at a time. Then you may choose to call forward multiple people at once to speed up the process beginning with the fourth generation back. For your grandparents, you will have four total cards, and they will each have their own basket full of energy that you will hand to them. Your great-grandparents will consist of four individuals on each side of your genetic lineage, or eight individuals total, and again they will each have their own baskets of energy passed back.

When you get to four generations back, your great-great-grandparents will have eight individuals on each side, or a total of sixteen. Beginning here, you can combine all of the individuals in the generation into two cards, one representing your mother's lineage and the other your father's. The number of individuals on each side doubles with every generation backward through your lineage, so you may continue to work through your ancestors until you reach seven generations back into your genetic lineage. Once you have completed working through seven generations of ancestors, you will then ask your guides to place any remaining energies from eight generations back and beyond into your basket and pass those back to whomever they belong to.

The following is a list of cards representing your ancestors and the combined generations you will want to create to work through:

1st Generation
(2 cards)
Mother, Father

2nd Generation - Grandparents
(4 cards)
Mother's Mother, Mother's Father, Father's Mother,
Father's Father

3rd Generation - Great-Grandparents
(8 cards)
Mother's Mother's Mother, Mother's Mother's Father,
Mother's Father's Mother, Mother's Father's Father,
Father's Mother's Mother, Father's Mother's Father,
Father's Father's Mother, Father's Father's Father

4th Generation - Great-Great-Grandparents
(2 cards)
Great-Great-Grandparents on Mother's Side (8)
Great-Great-Grandparents on Father's Side (8)

5th Generation - Great-Great-Great-Grandparents
(2 cards)

Great-Great-Great-Grandparents on Mother's Side (16)
Great-Great-Great-Grandparents on Father's Side (16)

6th Generation - 4x Great-Grandparents
(2 cards)
4x Great-Grandparents on Mother's Side (32)
4x Great-Grandparents on Father's Side (32)

7th Generation - 5x Great-Grandparents
(2 cards)
5x Great-Grandparents on Mother's Side (64)
5x Great-Grandparents on Father's Side (64)

8th Generation and Beyond
(1 card)
All of my genetic relations more than seven generations back

This process can take quite a bit of time, so it can be most helpful to tackle this healing in parts and to spread it out over the course of days or weeks. Use your intuition and your heart's guidance to help you move through this process in timing that is perfect for you, and always do your post-healing self-care practices to ensure that you manage the release of energy in the most easeful way possible.

It is also helpful to keep a chart or journal to track which parts of your lineage you have worked through. You may use the ancestral wheel included on the opposite page to track your progress. This wheel outlines all of the biological relatives in your genetic family lineage. It is an excellent tool for keeping track of ancestral energies, tuning into specific branches of your lineage intuitively, or for charting the genealogy of your genetic lineage.

7 GENERATIONS
ANCESTRAL WHEEL

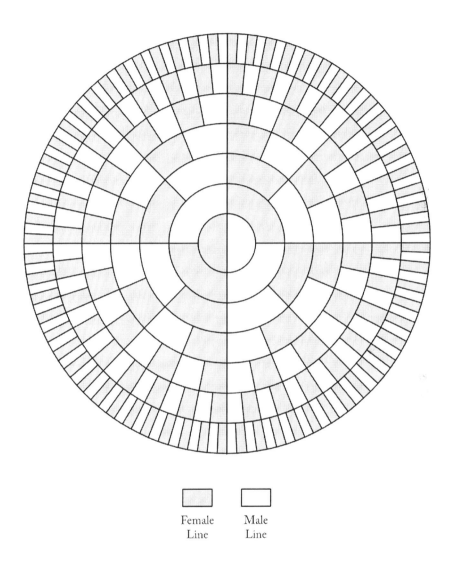

Female
Line

Male
Line

With yourself in the center of the wheel, trace your lineage outward. Each generation is represented by a ring of the circle. Each segment represents a single person in your lineage.

This exercise works because it addresses all parts of the ROESA Method and meets the prerequisites for healing all in one exercise. By visualizing a basement full of things that do not belong to us, we are seeing a metaphor or a representation of the ancestral energies that we are wanting to release. We see what is *real*. As we work through passing energies back to each ancestor, we witness the root of these energies. We find the *origin*. When we ask to see what is in the basket and feel the weight of its contents on us, we understand the influence of these energies on our current experience to whatever degree is necessary. We see the *effect*. From here, we simply need to decide that we want to release the ancestral trauma energies that are not serving us. With this, we determine how we want to *shift* things. Finally, we *authorize* Spirit to remove what is weighing us down in a balanced way, and our guides take care of the rest.

As you work through this healing, make note of any shifts that you experience in your life and your feeling state in the following days and weeks. You may notice yourself feeling lighter and more uplifted. You may notice that certain experiences or tasks feel easier to you, or that certain negative patterns or events begin to fall away. Whatever your experience is, this preliminary ancestral trauma release is a simple, but significant step toward reclaiming sovereignty over your energy body and healing your ancestral burdens.

As a healer it is not our job to do others' healing for them. We are only truly meant to support an individual through their own healing process, but only if they desire that healing and if it is in our highest good to do so. This support can manifest in many different ways. Sometimes this means we have to be firm and set boundaries, even with our ancestors, and other times this means we step in to ask for guidance and support from Spirit on an ancestor's behalf. While it may feel challenging to embody a "tough love" attitude in some cases, it is important to know that this healing will only ever work in a way that serves the growth and highest good of all.

It is also important to remember that challenges, people, and patterns in our own lives are attracted to us by the energies within us, even if these energies do not belong to us. Returning these ancestral trauma energies to their source allows us to begin attracting a new more aligned experience, and gives us more space to heal our own trauma, which is something we *are* responsible for.

๛

PERSONAL TRAUMA HEALING

There are two primary reasons we experience personal trauma. The first is because a traumatic experience is magnetized to us through the presence of foreign or ancestral trauma energies in our energy field. The second is that we may have agreed to experience certain traumas in order to learn and grow from the process of overcoming and healing them. Either way, the higher reason for our traumatic experiences can be a hard pill to swallow.

Throughout my healing process I often grappled with the "why" behind my traumatic childhood experiences. Had I done something in a past life that attracted these experiences to me? Had I failed to act in certain ways as a child that could have prevented further trauma? Did I deserve my experience for one reason or another? It's really easy to blame ourselves or explore ways that things could have been different when we begin to fully see the imbalances and traumas that have impacted our lives so deeply.

It wasn't until I had fully alchemized my childhood traumas and moved on with my life that my guides shared some of the reasons for my most challenging life experiences and relationships with me. None of these reasons involved blame, shame, or fault on my part, and while I would never wish to experience my life's challenges again, I have come to see how my experiences and healing from them have benefited me in profound ways.

I have found this to also be true for many of the clients I have worked with as well. I have yet to meet someone who has experienced trauma or challenges in life because they are deserving of it or are being punished for past actions in some way. Instead, our experiences, no matter how challenging to overcome, are often the perfect avenue to learn, grow, resolve imbalances in our being, and activate our soul wisdom and purpose in life when we choose the path of healing.

Regardless of the reasons we experience our traumas, they are a critical component of our ancestral healing journey. Even if the traumas we have experienced are unrelated to ancestral burdens we have inherited, the impact of our trauma becomes a part of our Ancestral Blueprint and its impact can then be passed down to future generations and future lifetimes that we live. As unfair as it may seem, no matter what our traumas are or who was involved in our experience of them, it is our responsibility to repair the imbalances left behind by those experiences.

There are many ways to work through trauma healing, but to fully release the energy from trauma and repair the internal fracturing that created it, the five prerequisites for healing must be met. One way we can do this is through a simple meditative exercise with the help of our guides.

To begin, find a comfortable and quiet place where you feel safe and can work through this exercise undisturbed. Once you are comfortable, call your spiritual support team forward to assist you with this personal trauma healing. You can say something like:

I call upon my guides, higher self, and Spirit to assist me with fully releasing any personal traumas and their impact that are in my highest good to release at this time.

Next, close your eyes and ask your higher self to bring forth a memory of an experience that created trauma energy for you that would be beneficial for you to heal now. Allow a memory to come forth and trust whatever comes to mind, regardless of what the experience is. This memory will play out in your mind until it is complete. Once the entire scope of the memory has been brought to your awareness, choose an impactful scene from this memory and imagine it as a photograph in your hands. This photograph represents the experience and all of the trauma energies, emotional energies, limiting beliefs, and patterns that were created as a result of this experience.

With this photograph in your hand, imagine a fire in front of you. When you feel ready, burn the photograph in your mind's eye with the intention that the limiting energies from this experience be released from your being.

Once the photo is burned to ashes, it's time to get creative. Your next step is to write a new scene, or a new memory, of what you experienced. This new scene can be completely unrealistic or improbable, but it is your scene to create and it is important that you create it in a way that honors your boundaries, your truth, and that does no harm to yourself or others. When working through this step, think about what words you would like to speak that you perhaps didn't get to. Reflect on what words you would like to hear spoken to you that were never spoken. How can this scene play out differently so that it does not create trauma energy or a fracturing experience for you? Spend as much time as you need making your new scene, and feel how this new memory feels in your body.

Just like the first scene, your next step is to imagine a photograph in your hand that represents this new scene you have written. Once the photograph is in hand, imagine a bulletin board in front of you. This bulletin board represents your being and the information that will inform it from here forward. When you feel ready, pin your new photograph to this bulletin board.

With this step complete, you can now give your guides permission to clear any energies from your being that are not in alignment with this new scene. You can say something like:

I give permission to my guides to clear any trauma energies, emotional energies, limiting beliefs, limiting programs, limiting intentions, connections, and other harmful energies that are not in alignment with my new healed story.

Any time we release something from our being and our Ancestral Blueprint, it is important to replace it with something more uplifting. To do this, you can request that your guides give you new energies that are in alignment with your core truth or your soul's truth. You can say something like:

I give permission to my guides to replace any of these energies I have released with new uplifting energies, belief templates, and programs that are in alignment with my soul's truth.

Give yourself plenty of time to release and receive, and check in with yourself to see how this healing feels in your body. If you feel you can work through more personal traumas, you may repeat this exercise with another memory. If you need time to process this first trauma release, take a break and perform your self-care routine.

It can be extremely helpful to integrate this exercise into your regular spiritual or healing practice as it will allow you to mindfully work through and release significant amounts of trauma energy. Pace yourself and always trust your inner guidance as to how frequently to work through this exercise. Also be aware that as the energies from this exercise release, you may feel them on the way out, so it can lead to emotional release or other symptoms of healing for hours or days after completing this exercise. Ensure that you have the proper personal and professional support in place to help you process these memories as they come up, and never work through too much at once.

❧

PAST LIFE TRAUMA HEALING

The more we explore ourselves, our internal world, and our past experiences, the more we understand the nature of our being. Consciously working to transform the patterns and energies that are not in alignment with our soul-self is alchemy at its finest. Through this work, we become masters of change and conscious creators of our life experiences. We begin weeding the garden, keeping what belongs to us, and releasing what does not. Every so often, though, we are caught by surprise. We confront something that seems foreign and mysterious, yet its roots run deep and it grabs us at our core.

Part of the magic of incarnation is the forgetting process we go through when we come into each life. This forgetting of our past allows us to have an experience that feels new to us. We are then able to isolate and work through specific themes and embark on a new mission in each lifetime without the confusion that would come from remembering past identities and personalities that we embodied. Just because we can't remember the entire scope of our soul's experiences doesn't mean they didn't happen and that the impact of those experiences isn't still with us.

We are often able to balance the traumatic experiences that we have had in past lifetimes after the life is complete; however, in certain cases we must learn through new physical experiences to fully understand and balance our past life challenges. In the same way that our genetic ancestral burdens influence the trajectory of our lives, our past life traumas and resulting patterns can bleed through into our current experience if they have not been healed. We will then experience fear, trauma, and different patterns in our current lifetime that reflect the same themes of our unresolved past.

Past life healing seems challenging enough if we can accept the concept of past life trauma impacting our current experience, but there are many people out there who do not believe in past lives. This seems like it might throw a wrench in their healing process. Even if we do believe in past lives, it might seem impossible to heal from something that we don't remember from a lifetime that we are not currently living. Regardless of our belief in past lives, there are many avenues to healing the burdens we bring with us from our soul's past. Spirit does not discriminate, and will always provide a path toward healing that aligns with each individual's ability to understand and gather the resources necessary to heal.

There are many ways to access the burdens that we bring with us from our past lifetimes. Past life regressions are effective at guiding us intuitively to information that can be helpful for healing past life traumas, and it is possible to do regressive past life healing exercises on our own with success. For those who have never attempted this type of work before, though, regressions are typically best done with the support of a trained healer, coach, or therapist.

Regardless of our understanding of past lives or our ability to access them, we can also begin to explore the energies impacting us from our past by directly reflecting on the prerequisites for healing. We can use a simple process to meet the prerequisites and work with our spiritual support team to help us transform the patterns that we recognize and understand.

You can begin this process by gathering a pen and paper for a reflective journaling exercise. The first step is to choose a fear that you can recognize within yourself. Ask your guides and higher self to help bring to your mind a fear that would be most helpful to release at this time. Once you identify a fear, you have met the first prerequisite for healing - naming what is real.

Our next step is to trace this fear to its origin. It may be from a past life or it may be from an experience in this life. You may remember the origin of the fear, or you may not. Your goal here is to do the best you can and to be as specific as you can. In some cases this might mean you can identify that your fear developed during a past life in the 1600's when you lost a family member unexpectedly. In other cases, you might only know that the fear comes from some point in your childhood in this life.

To work through this step, ask yourself, "What times in my current life have I experienced this fear?" Make a list of every specific memory and experience that comes to your mind. Do you notice any themes or similarities between each of these experiences? How far back in your life do they go? Can you identify the first time you felt this fear in your life, or do you feel as if you have always had this fear from the time you were born? Are there any specific traumas you can think of in your past that may have contributed to the creation of this fear? Does anyone else in your genetic family have this same fear, or is it exclusive to you? Answering these questions can help you narrow down the origin of the fear as much as possible, and this meets the second prerequisite for healing.

Next, we must assess the effect that this fear is having on your current life experience. What actions are you unable to take because of this fear that you would like to take? What actions do you take because of this fear that you would rather not take? How does the triggering of this fear prevent you from living the life you want to live? If this fear did not exist, how would your life be different? Understanding how our fears shape the way we navigate life is a very important step toward healing. This allows us to grab hold of our fear and see it for what it is. It encourages a recognition that the fear we are working with is not a natural part of us, but rather a reaction to a traumatic experience that we may or may not remember. With this understanding, we have met the third prerequisite for healing.

Our next step is to decide how we would like to shift things. Spend some time reflecting on what you would like your life to be like without this fear present. It may be helpful to choose an experience from your past where this fear arose and rewrite the story, just like we did in the previous exercise. Ask yourself how your life will feel more free once this fear is gone.

Once you have worked through the first four prerequisites, you now have the power to authorize change. Your only remaining job is to give your spiritual support team permission to clear any energies that stand between you and your new vision for yourself. You can use a statement similar to the following to complete this process:

Guides, higher self, and Spirit, I give permission to you now to clear any trauma energies, emotional energies, limiting beliefs, limiting programs, limiting intentions, or other energies from my current life and any past life experiences I have had that are not in alignment with the complete release of this fear and my new vision for myself. I give permission to replace anything cleared with energies and templates that are in alignment with my core truth and highest path in life.

Allow these energies to clear from your body and notice any sensations or feelings that arise as they release. Make sure to practice your post-healing self-care routine after working through this process, and be mindful that this release can continue after the exercise is complete.

While the experiences we have that create and perpetuate trauma can be very complex, our process for healing them does not need to be. In some cases, we may be guided to witness past life events in order to heal them, and if this is the case we will be guided to the appropriate resources. In other cases, we may need to rewrite the story of our trauma to create a new path for ourselves. We might even need to set some boundaries and pass back what does not belong to us. Even a simple self-reflection exercise can have a powerful healing impact when we understand the requirements for healing. When we work with Spirit and give permission to release the parts of our past that no longer serve us, a simple exercise can allow us to make significant progress toward positive change. Once the energy of our unbalanced past is released, our lives can coalesce around a new positive potential that is informed by the authentic expression of our soul-self.

Chapter 5

Overcoming Limiting Patterns

W orking to heal and release ancestral trauma alone has a very significant positive impact on our healing. Our ancestral trauma creates and is the anchor for our other ancestral burdens, so working to heal and transform the trauma energies within us releases us from the limiting experiences we have as a result of trauma. When we heal trauma, we give permission to embody a new authentic truth, and in doing so we repair the internal fracturing caused by the original traumatic experience. This is powerful healing for ourselves and our lineage.

While it is possible to identify many of the trauma energies we hold in our energy field, some of them can become so integrated into our experience that they seem elusive. This is especially true if the trauma that impacts us has been present since before our birth into this life, or if we have no memory of the trauma we have personally experienced. Despite the challenges that we might have in attempting to identify trauma, there are always clues that can lead us to the places in our Ancestral Blueprint that need attention, and these clues can come in the form of the limiting patterns that we experience in our lives.

Limiting patterns are our second category of ancestral burden, and they can only be created through the presence of trauma energy. This means that identifying and working to heal our limiting patterns is an entry point we can use to guide us to any unresolved ancestral or personal trauma we might have. Everything is connected and there are many ways to navigate the imbalances in our Ancestral Blueprint.

When we have unbalanced energies in our Ancestral Blueprint, our experiences reflect the effects of those imbalances and we often experience challenge and conflict. While it may not always feel like it, life is always working in our favor, and the circumstances we manifest through our unbalanced energies are always designed to help us achieve balance. When we follow the path of healing, we can begin to use our challenges to identify the limiting patterns that we think, feel, and act through, trace them to their origin, assess their impact, and start the healing process.

The limiting patterns we can have in our Ancestral Blueprint come in two forms, the first of which are limiting belief templates. These are energetic templates that anchor into our experience the sentiment and the subsequent effect of beliefs we develop through trauma. Our beliefs shape our entire perception of reality, so working to transform limiting beliefs changes the way we experience our lives internally and what we can manifest in our lives externally.

Even if we can identify limiting beliefs that we hold, we often try to change these beliefs by forcing our thoughts, emotions, and behavioral patterns into a new state through repetition of thought or action. This can be a temporary solution if we repeat a new pattern often enough. However, without addressing the trauma and the energetic templates that are the root cause of our limiting beliefs, there is always a potential for falling back into old patterns. All it takes is a triggering experience and all of the hard work we have done to try to shift old patterns falls to the wayside and our old patterns come racing back to the forefront.

When we work with our limiting beliefs on the energetic template level of our being, we can stop old patterns at their origin. This work then allows our thoughts, neural pathways, emotions, behaviors, and choices to fall into alignment with new beliefs that are not based on the limitations and traumatic experiences of the past. This makes this form of healing extremely powerful and much easier than taking our beliefs on by force. When we transform the energy first, we ensure that the physical experience we have will match our consciously created energetic templates.

☙

HEALING LIMITING BELIEFS

Awareness is key when it comes to permanently healing our limiting patterns, regardless of whether they come from our own life experiences or through our lineage. Becoming aware of our limiting beliefs is the first step toward healing, as they are the entry point into this healing work. This can be a challenge, especially if our family, peers, or culture hold these same limiting beliefs. It often takes contrast to show us that something exists beyond what we have thought to be true in the past.

Our challenges, lower emotions, and triggering experiences are a great place to start when we begin looking for the limiting beliefs we might be operating through. If an experience we have doesn't feel good or uplifting for us, this is a big clue that something is out of balance. Try to think of an experience that caused you to feel fearful, insecure, angry, or judgmental toward yourself or others. Ask yourself, "What story am I telling myself that reinforces my negative emotions that may not be true?"

Your answer to this question likely reflects a limiting belief template that is influencing your thoughts, emotions, and behaviors.

Once we know what limiting belief we want to work with, we've identified what is real. We know that we have a limiting belief template and what the sentiment of that limiting belief is. We know that trauma contributed to the formation of this belief, whether it be our own trauma, an ancestor's trauma, or both. We also know that we may have other limiting patterns, repressed emotional energies, and other energies in our energy field that reflect and reinforce the intent of this limiting belief.

Our next step is to identify the origin of this limiting belief. In some cases, it might suffice to simply know that some trauma from the past is the origin. It can be helpful, though, to reflect on the limiting belief and consider where it came from. Did someone teach this belief to you? Was it someone from your genetic lineage? Did you have an experience in the past that caused you to form this belief? Ask Spirit to help you trace the origin of this belief and journal about all of the experiences that come to mind that have served to reinforce this limiting belief you have.

With the origin of the belief determined, you can now move on to the next prerequisite for healing, which is to identify how this limiting belief is impacting your experience. Spend some time thinking about how this belief has limited you. Ask yourself if there are different choices you might have made in your past if this limiting belief did not exist. Think about all of the ways your emotions, your thoughts, and your actions have been informed by this limiting belief.

With this in mind, you can begin to work toward creating a new belief template that honors your core truth. To do this, write a new belief statement that feels true to you and that reflects a positive and loving sentiment. This can be in the format of a mantra or positive affirmation, and can be as simple or detailed as you like. In writing this statement, you are deciding how you want things to shift moving forward, and you can now use this statement to clear the energies in your Ancestral Blueprint that are limiting for you with the help of Spirit.

To begin the healing process, read the positive statement you have written out loud or in your mind. Once you read your new positive statement, you can now call forth your spiritual support team and ask them to use this statement to clear limiting energies in your Ancestral Blueprint and energy body, and to replace your limiting belief templates with templates that reflect your authentic truth. This will effectively remove not only the limiting belief templates that conflict with your positive statement, but the emotions and trauma energies that anchor them in place too. You can state something like:

I give permission to my guides, higher self, and Spirit to clear any emotional energy, trauma energy, limiting beliefs, limiting programs, limiting intentions, and other energies that are not in alignment with this positive statement. I request that these energies be cleared now and replaced with templates and energies that are in alignment with my core truth.

The clearing will begin as soon as this permission is given, and you may feel energy moving in your body or experience energy clearing symptoms. Because this exercise addresses all of the prerequisites for healing and removes all of the energies and templates that are connected to the original trauma, the pattern can no longer repeat. In the following days and weeks after this healing, you will begin to notice shifts in your emotions and thinking. They will begin to reflect a more positive outlook rather than being informed by the limiting patterns of the past. Once you take a physical action or have a new physical experience through the lens of this healed and authentic belief template, the template is then activated and will be the primary sentiment that informs your experience from here forth.

You may repeat this exercise regularly as part of your healing practice, or any time you become aware of a limiting belief or pattern that is operating within you. If you need help getting started, try this healing process using the three example positive belief statements below and then give permission to your spiritual support team to release energies that are not in alignment with these statements:

Example 1: I am not limited by the patterns, life circumstances, and choices of my genetic lineage, family members, or soul lineage. I am free to live my life as I choose, and I am capable of great achievement, abundance, and fulfillment in my life.

Example 2: While I am capable of healing my ancestral lineages within myself and for myself, and while my healing has a positive and healing effect on my ancestral connections, I am not responsible for the life choices, behavior, healing, lack of healing, beliefs, traumas, or patterns that exist in my ancestral lineages outside of myself. It is not my responsibility to ensure that those in my genetic lineage grow and heal, for just as I have the free will choice to do my healing, they have the free will choice to experience life as they choose. My responsibility is to do healing within myself and to live my life in a way that exemplifies that healing.

Example 3: My value and worth are innate. They come from my existence and my existence alone. There are no actions or achievements that change my worth or value for better or worse. My appearance, financial resources, beliefs, affiliations, age, gender, sexual expression, capabilities and talents, and any other expressions of myself have no bearing on my worth or value. My worth is infinite and immeasurable. My value is beyond human comprehension. No person or being determines my worth, and any opinions that others have about me, good or bad, have no bearing on my worth or value. I am equal to all of creation. I am powerful and sovereign, and I love myself and have compassion for myself unconditionally always.

Writing our own belief statements empowers us to see and experience life through a more authentic and truthful lens. When we work with Spirit to request healing, we bring our positive affirmations and intentions to an entirely new level. The repetition of positive affirmations is not necessary when we do this work to clear the energies and templates that anchor our limiting beliefs in place. The impact of this healing work can be felt and experienced almost immediately, and while it is work, it is productive work that leads to positive change for us and our ancestors.

IDENTIFYING LIMITING PROGRAMS

The second form of limiting patterns we can have in our Ancestral Blueprint are limiting programs. Limiting programs are created through the limiting beliefs that we have, and are similar to limiting beliefs in that they are informed by trauma. These limiting programs run in our energy field and cause certain automatic emotions, thoughts, behaviors, or physical responses to unfold based on the intention of the program. They tell us that if a certain thing happens, then we will react in this certain way. They are a result of the presence of limiting beliefs, and they are activated by specific events or experiences that reflect the trauma that exists in our Ancestral Blueprint and energy field.

So, how do our traumas, limiting beliefs, and limiting programs work in our lives? Well, let's look at an example. Perhaps as a young child, you are walking down the sidewalk eating a cookie. Out of nowhere, a man with a mustache comes running up from behind and bumps you on his way down the sidewalk. You fall down, skin your knees and hands, and your cookie is ruined. This is a painful experience, so a part of you unconsciously decides that men with mustaches are dangerous, will hurt you, and will destroy the things you are enjoying.

This experience creates a fracturing within you because the new belief you have created through this experience is not in alignment with your core truth, and is informed by this traumatic experience. Your fractured child-self that is informed by this trauma decides that some protective measures should be implemented to ensure that this doesn't happen again. As a result, a couple of energetic programs are created. One says something like, "If I see a man with a mustache, then I will get away as fast as I can." Another says, "If I am eating something I really like, then I should be particularly wary of my surroundings." You now have trauma energy, a limiting belief template, and limiting programs that are linked to one another and that inform your experience.

Fast forward to the future. As an adult, you may notice that you feel anxious and have a heightened sense of awareness or nervous system activation whenever you eat a cookie or something else you enjoy. You may have an aversion toward men with mustaches or even feel as if you want to run away when you see a mustache. You might avoid dating perfectly nice men who have mustaches because the part of you that has been informed by this experience believes they are dangerous.

None of these future experiences that are informed by the trauma, limiting beliefs, and programs will feel good. They will cause you to feel dysregulated in your nervous system, you may experience lower emotions or anxiety, and you may act in ways or make choices that prevent you from having positive and uplifting experiences. This is how trauma energy and limiting patterns impact us on a personal level, yet it doesn't stop here.

If this experience happened to us in a past life or to one of our ancestors and was left unhealed, we may end up exhibiting these same beliefs, programs, and behaviors in our own life with no idea where they came from. Without addressing these ancestral burdens energetically, we may go our entire life struggling to enjoy food that we find enjoyable and fearing men with mustaches because of an experience our great-grandmother had. This is the impact that ancestral burdens can have on us.

To begin identifying limiting programs, it can be helpful to reflect on any cause-and-effect patterns that you notice in your life. These patterns can be with behaviors that you have, autonomic physiological responses, or repetitive actions that you take. Programs in our Ancestral Blueprint tell us to do a certain thing when another thing happens, and the limiting programs we have cause us to repeat thoughts, emotions, and behaviors that are not beneficial for us.

You can start by asking yourself a series of questions to get an idea of what programs might be running in your Ancestral Blueprint. Are there any go-to actions you take when you are feeling emotionally triggered? Do you shut down and isolate, do you get anxious, do you lash out, or do you overeat or stop eating? If a certain event or circumstance appears in your life, do you always handle it in a certain way without thinking about it? Do you have a certain habit or routine that you do without thinking about it that may not be serving you well? Your answers to any of these questions may point to programs you have running in your energy field or Ancestral Blueprint.

To get started, try reflecting on the following general examples of program types and notice if anything from your own life comes to mind:

> - *Programs that cause your nervous system to become activated when you see, hear, or feel certain things*
> - *Programs that cause you to take a certain unhelpful action at a certain time of day*
> - *Programs that cause you to think certain thoughts in a certain situation*
> - *Programs that were created due to past traumas that have already been healed and are no longer helpful*

Once you identify a program that you think you might have, think about how that program might be reflective of a limiting belief. Think about any personal or ancestral traumas that may have contributed to the creation of this program. Reflecting on this can help you identify the entire scope of the program.

At this point, you can use a clearing statement to remove any limiting programs you think you might have and other connected energies by using a clearing statement. You can say something like:

I give permission to my guides, higher self, and Spirit to clear any programs that cause me to (x) when (y) happens and any emotional energy, trauma energy, limiting beliefs, other limiting programs, limiting intentions, and other energies that contribute to the continuation of this program running in my being. I request that these energies be cleared now and replaced with templates and energies that are in alignment with my core truth.

Adjust this statement so that (x) matches the impact of the program, and (y) so that it matches the trigger of the program.

Once the program removal healing is complete, you should begin to notice that you react in new ways when faced with old situations. Your reactions become less automatic and more reflective of the balanced state of your authentic self.

Limiting pattern healing work shows us that we can use any ancestral burdens we can identify to remove the trauma energies that created them in the first place. We can navigate our ancestral burdens through a variety of entry points that all guide us to the root of our limitations and lead to healing. This work is how we free ourselves from the burdens that prevent our most authentic expression of self from coming through, and it is how we offer our lineage the opportunity to do the same.

Chapter 6

Healing Limiting Intentions

For beginners and experts alike, the most important principle in energy healing is that all energy moves because our attention is placed upon someone or something, and our intention then transforms whatever our attention is placed upon in some way. We can't take a walk outside until we place our attention on what exists outside of our door and then set an intention to get up and go wherever it is our attention lands. We also can't clear an emotional block, limiting belief, trauma, or other energy unless we are aware that it exists and intend to release it. Intention creates change, transformation, and movement in both freeing ways and in ways that limit us.

Most of us walk around all day, completely unaware of the limitations that we experience in our thoughts, emotions, and actions. We are so accustomed to the ways we are limited that we often need a very triggering or catalyzing experience to bring our attention to the energies and experiences that are not serving us well. If you've ever seen someone red-faced and frothing at the mouth yell, "I'M NOT ANGRY!," you get exactly what I'm talking about.

Because of this lack of awareness that humanity often suffers from, we have no idea how our intentions are impacting ourselves and others. Intention is extremely powerful. It is the force of creative change, but when we are unaware of the power that our intentions yield, we can easily find ourselves throwing them about without a real understanding of their impact. We can also be caught blindsided by the limiting intentions that others have for us and the impact that these intentions can have on our lives.

Intention is tricky because it isn't physical. It is the precursor to action and it is how we take aim toward something. This makes it easy for us to be unaware of how our intentions impact things. We see the physical result of intention all around us, but we never stop to think about what manifests all of these physical experiences we keep having. Everything is a manifestation of the combined intentions of everyone who has placed attention upon that thing. We physically exist as a living human because the intentions our ancestors had generations before we were even a thought led to the opportunity for our birth.

When we shift our focus from the physical experience we are having to the intentions that led to the physical experience, we begin to see the code that makes up the program. If the program isn't working the way we want it to, there is most certainly code behind the scenes in the form of a limiting intention that has created our experience. Sometimes we were the programmer, and sometimes it was someone else, but no matter who created the limiting intentions that are impacting our lives in ways that we don't like, we always have the power to write some new code.

Regardless of whether our intentions appear to manifest in physical form or not, they always manifest into energetic potential. Intentions combined with any form of energy create energetic structures. These energetic structures could remain in the realms of possibility and never impact our experience at all, they may pack enough punch to influence other energies such as thoughts, emotions, or beliefs, and they may also certainly become a part of our physical experience. When we only take life at face value, though, we miss all of the energetic influences and intentions that lead to our experiences. When we don't know what causes something, we have a very difficult time changing it.

The impact that intentions have is timeless. Nothing is isolated, and anything that manifests through intention has a ripple effect. Intention locks patterns and other energies into place until another intention changes the status quo. Unless we become aware of the intentions from the past that may be limiting us in some way, we are stuck with the effects of those intentions until we can consciously create change.

It might seem a bit unfair that the intentions of others can influence our lives in such profound ways, but there are a few caveats with external influence. We can never be influenced by limiting intentions unless we have something within ourselves that is energetically in agreement with the influence. If someone directs any form of limiting intention toward us and we have no traumas, repressed emotions, limiting beliefs, unconscious intentions of our own, or other resonant energies in our energy field, then the energetic structure created by the limiting intention cannot stick. When we do our inner healing work and overcome our wounds and challenges, any limiting intentions of our own or from others that influence us fall away because there is nothing in resonance with them any longer. Any form of inner healing work, regardless of the approach used to achieve it, has the side effect of clearing limiting intentions of any kind that are related to the healing.

This might seem like the best approach to overcoming limiting intentions, and it certainly is the most common path that most people take, but sometimes the limiting intentions that affect us themselves make it very difficult to overcome them. Their influence often causes us to see life through the lens of limiting intentions rather than our own truth, which is why we can have a very difficult time seeing that we have the option to change things. It can take a tremendous amount of challenge to shake us around and wake us up enough to see the forest through the trees.

The energetic structures created by limiting intentions can take countless different forms. For the sake of our work with ancestral healing, two of the most important of these energetic structures are contracts and curses.

Energetic contracts are agreements that we make with ourselves and other individuals. Some of these contracts, such as our soul contract, are very beneficial and even critical to life. We can also make contracts through the lens of our fears, traumas, limiting beliefs, and limiting programming that are detrimental to us and prevent us from living life in the ways that we desire.

Ancestral contracts can be between us and a single other person from our lineage, or they can be between us and the lineage itself. Ancestral contracts with specific individuals are often made with our living relatives through our interactions with them. They could be something like a parent giving a child money, as long as the child takes certain actions or agrees to certain conditions. These conditions might be unspoken and unwritten, but they exist through the combined intentions of the parent and the child nonetheless. These conditions may not be in the highest good of the child and may block the child from expressing themselves and living their life authentically and purposefully.

We may also have contracts with our entire lineage. Perhaps we are born into a lineage that expects us to remain in a certain location for our entire life. This contract may activate through our birth into the lineage, and we may find it very emotionally and physically difficult to move to another place when we become an adult. We might feel anxious every time we leave our hometown, or we might run into obstacles like canceled flights or a rental falling through at the last minute. Our life can be shaped by the intentions of contracts that were created in our lineage long before we were alive, and this can make it difficult to track the cause of our woes if we never bother to look at the energy behind them.

Our ancestral contracts are not limited to our genetic lineage either. We can create contracts with ourselves in past lives that are meant to prevent us from taking certain actions or making certain choices. This usually happens because we have experienced some form of trauma, pain, or suffering, and because of that experience, we make a very strong commitment to ourselves to never have that experience again. This can cause problems because each lifetime occurs in a different era with different people and different conditions, so something that may have been harmful in one lifetime may not be in another.

Many healers often find that they have a deep fear of their intuition or of energy work that they have to overcome. If they look into their Ancestral Blueprint they often find that they were persecuted for doing healing work in a past life where "magic" and natural healing were considered witchcraft, which was a punishable offense. This is most often not the case any longer, but an agreement with oneself to never do healing work again can be difficult to overcome regardless of the actual life circumstances of a person because the fear that arises is very real.

Becoming aware of contracts and their influence, and then choosing to change or destroy them, is a powerful way to claim sovereignty over our lives. We are only stuck in a contract energetically if we don't know that it exists and therefore aren't aware that we can take action to change it.

We can begin to identify limiting contracts by looking at

places in our lives where we feel blocked and unable to move forward, despite our desire and efforts to make change. If our intentions and actions are not moving us in the direction we want to go, there could be a contract or other form of limiting intention in place that we are not aware of that needs to be cleared first. If limiting intentions are influencing us, we can forcibly overcome them in some cases, but not without a lot of struggle or hardship. Luckily, we have Spirit and our own conscious awareness on our side to help us clear any limiting contracts that are impacting us.

～

LIMITING CONTRACTS

The first step in clearing ancestral contracts is to identify a contract that exists. This can be done with some self-reflection and an awareness of certain unhealthy dynamics that you might have in your life. Ask yourself if there are any actions you take or ways that you behave that do not feel as if they are natural to you or the way that you are ideally wanting to behave. Are there certain areas of your life where you seem to give your power away, concede to someone else's wishes, or deny your own feelings and desires? Are there certain people or areas of your life that feel toxic to you, yet you feel trapped? Spend some time thinking about why certain conditions in your life exist and ask yourself what intentions made by yourself or others might have created these conditions.

We can also identify contracts by thinking through broad categories of life that might have limiting contracts attached to them. Think through the way you navigate money, politics, religion, relationships, intimacy, diet, exercise, communication, work, education, and other aspects of your life. Try to think of different contracts that you might have in each category and write them down so that you can begin to work with them.

Let's say you identify a contract that says that you will always tolerate abusive behavior for as long as the abusive person is supporting you financially. With this contract identified, the next step is to assess where this contract came from. Ask yourself with whom this contract has played out. Did you have this contract with one of your parents? Do you have any ancestors in past generations that you know may have exhibited this same behavior in relationships? If so, this could be an ancestral contract. If not, perhaps it is a personal contract that was created through a traumatic experience that you had in your own life. Tune into yourself and see if you can get a feeling or knowing as to where this contract originated.

After you get as close to the origin of the contract as possible, your next step is to identify how the intention of the contract is impacting you. In the example, this contract may be preventing you from leaving toxic relationships or may cause you to tolerate behavior from others that you certainly do not deserve. Think of any experiences you've had in your past that you feel may have been influenced by this contract. You can ask your higher self and guides to bring memories to your mind that may be associated with this contract.

Our fourth step before we can receive healing is to decide how we want to shift things. One of the most empowering ways we can do this is to write a new contract for ourselves. In our new contract, our goal is to free ourselves from the burden and limitations of any contracts we have identified. Similar to limiting belief statements from the previous chapter, we can make a statement of sovereignty that will serve as a guide for destroying limiting contracts we might have. If we take our example from above, perhaps we write a contract that says something like:

Abuse from any person or being is not allowed to be part of my reality for any reason or under any circumstance, including from those who financially support me. My circumstances, connections, and conditions will always coalesce to remove toxic and abusive people from my life in a safe way, and I will no longer hold any energies or patterns within me that support abusive treatment or toxic behavior in my life.

Once this affirming statement is written, it's time to make a choice. In the case of all forms of limiting intentions, we simply have to decide if we want to remove and destroy the energetic structure of the intention or if we want to keep being influenced by the limiting intention. The choice is always yours, but it's likely that you aren't really interested in being limited by intentions from the past if you are committed to healing. If that's the case, you can choose to destroy the contracts you have identified.

At this point, you can find a comfortable place to receive healing and call upon your spiritual support team to assist you in clearing any contracts with specific people or with your lineage that are not in alignment with your new contract or sovereignty statement. You can say something like:

I call upon my guides, higher self, and Spirit to assist me with a healing to destroy any contracts with my mother's side of my genetic lineage that cause me to tolerate abusive behavior for as long as the abusive person is financially supporting me. I ask that all contracts that are not in align-ment with my new statement of sovereignty and that are in my highest good to remove be destroyed now.

With your spiritual support team assisting you, close your eyes for a meditative exercise and visualize a stack of paper that represents the contracts you are destroying in front of you. The stack may be stories tall or a single piece of paper. Trust whatever you see, and when you feel ready, burn the stack of paper with the intention that you are destroying all of the contracts with the limiting sentiment. You can ask your guides or Spirit to assist you if you need help burning the contracts.

Next, you will give your guides permission to clear any energies that were anchored in place by these contracts and any energies that allowed these contracts to be created in the first place. Contract work of this kind is an excellent entry point into releasing all kinds of other limiting energies. You may say something like:

Guides, please clear any trauma energies, emotional energies, limiting belief templates, limiting programs, other limiting intentions, harmful connections, and any other limiting energies that were anchored in place by these contracts or that contributed to their creation.

Allow the energies to clear from your body for as long as you need to. You will then ask your guides to replace any removed energies and templates with those that are in your highest good. You may say something like:

Guides, please replace any removed energies or templates with energies and templates that are in my highest good to receive at this time and that are in alignment with my soul's truth.

This completes the healing, and moving forward you should be much more capable of acting through your own truth rather than the influences of the contracts you cleared. In the case of our example, this might mean that you are able to realize that it is not in your best interest to stay in certain toxic relationships. You may stand up for yourself more easily when others are behaving in a toxic way. You may even realize that you can forgive someone for their toxic behavior while simultaneously refusing to allow that pattern of behavior to exist in your life anymore. Contract work is very deep healing work, and the effects of it can be instantly transformative for very sticky and ingrained themes.

❧
ANCESTRAL CURSES

Ancestral curses and other forms of cursing work in much the same way as limiting contracts. Curses are another form of limiting intention that can influence us, but unlike contracts, they are often not something that we have agreed to consciously. The reason they are able to influence us at all is that we have a trauma, limiting belief, or other energy that is in resonance with the curse. If someone has an intention that we fail at something and this intention is strong enough to create an energetic structure that is then directed at us, it cannot stick to our energy unless we perhaps have a belief on some level that we are a failure in certain ways. If we are able to heal our belief that we are a failure, the curse will fall away on its own regardless of whether we are aware of it or not.

Ancestral curses can impact our lineage in two different ways. The first is if a specific individual is influenced by a curse and then has a subsequent traumatic experience as a result of the curse. The curse itself may not pass down through the lineage, but the impact of it can. This would include any emotions, trauma, limiting beliefs, programs, or other limiting energies that were created due to the curse. These limiting energies could then be passed down through a lineage and wreak havoc.

In other cases, curses themselves can be passed down through an ancestral lineage. These types of curses often only impact certain members of a family lineage such as all of the men, all of the firstborn children, or every other generation of an ancestral line. They can also be dormant and only activate if a certain condition is met, for example after a person in a lineage hits a certain age, after someone is married, or perhaps after the first trimester of a pregnancy. These types of curses can often be identified because of the unusual repetition of a pattern through an ancestral line that is unique to that lineage.

Ancestral curses are not limited to our genetic lineage and can pass down to us through our soul lineage as well. It is possible for others to curse us, for us to curse ourselves, and for the impact of that cursing to be felt if there is unresolved trauma energy that anchors the curse into our Ancestral Blueprint.

It might seem a bit strange that we would curse ourselves, but we do it all the time. Any time we tell ourselves that we aren't good enough, don't deserve the best, or treat ourselves unkindly in other ways, we could potentially be cursing ourselves. The energies created by these negative intentions we have toward ourselves have a real impact on our thoughts, emotions, and experiences.

Ancestral curses can come from a person inside our lineage, or can be placed on a lineage by an external source. In either case, once a curse finds its way into a lineage, it can leave a lot of damage in its wake. Just like other forms of limiting intentions that we might be influenced by, curses create challenges, conflict, trauma, and a lot of negativity, and it is important to attempt to break these cycles when we can.

To begin identifying curses, we can use similar self-reflection tactics to those we used for identifying contracts. Sometimes the words we use can be a great indicator of the presence of an energetic influence. Think of any events or circumstances in your life where you have struggled to change something or break out of a harmful pattern and thought to yourself, "I must be cursed." If the word pops up, this is a good place to start looking because it is likely that some part of you knows something is there even if you are not consciously aware of it.

We can begin the process of curse clearing by following the same process to work through the prerequisites for healing as we did in the previous exercise. No matter what form a limiting intention takes, it is important to use the ROESA Method to identify that it exists, what its origin is, how it's impacting us, decide how we want to change it, and give permission to clear it. Once these steps are complete, you can call in your spiritual support team, name what you suspect exists and is influencing you, and ask your guides to clear it. You can use language like:

Guides, higher self, and Spirit, please clear from my being any curses that come from my mother that are intended to make me suffer in the same ways that she did. Please also clear any emotions, trauma energies, limiting beliefs, limiting programs, contracts, connections, and other energies that are anchored in place by these curses or that contributed to their creation. Please replace any cleared energies and templates with those that are in my highest good and in alignment with my core truth.

There are many curses that are common in ancestral lineages, so it can be helpful to tackle some general intentions that might have resulted in a curse. It can be helpful to ask to clear each of these from your soul lineage and your genetic lineage separately. If you feel called to name a specific person or aspect of your genetic lineage that you feel might be the origin of a curse, you can work through the different possible origins separately as well. Try reflecting on and working through the following curse intentions. Notice if any of them cause you to recognize a pattern in your lineage as well as how you react to reading each one:

- *Curses intended to cause others to suffer in the same ways that the originator of the curse suffered*
- *Curses intended to limit free expression and ability to speak the truth*
- *Curses intended to keep younger generations beholden to the elders of the family*
- *Curses intended to cause premature death or illness*
- *Curses intended to cause financial loss or poverty*
- *Curses intended to prevent relatives from moving away from ancestral homelands*
- *Curses intended to impact only people of a certain gender in a lineage*
- *Curses intended to impact only individuals in a certain birth order*
- *Curses intended to limit or remove personal sovereignty*
- *Curses intended to limit or minimize intuitive abilities*

This exercise is an excellent way to start clearing any curses that exist with broad intentions. Once you feel comfortable with the process, try to tune into yourself and see if any limiting intentions come into your mind that might be more unique to you and your experience. Work through this same process, and make note of what you feel in your body as any energies are cleared.

Each lineage will be different in terms of what cursing and other limiting intentions are impacting it. The influence of limiting intentions very much depends on the amount of trauma and the amount of healing work that has occurred for the individuals in the lineage. For some individuals, limiting intention work is relatively easy. Others with more burdens in their Ancestral Blueprint might find an entire complex web of limiting intentions that lock them into certain patterns. No matter what the situation, it's important to know that these energies can be cleared and that there is no intention more powerful than our own. We are sovereign beings with free will, and it is only our own lack of awareness that keeps us limited.

✍
LIMITING INTENTION PREVENTION

As with many things, prevention is often the best way to reduce the harmful impact of anything. With an awareness of the impact that limiting intentions have on our physical reality, we can apply this awareness to our daily experiences and interactions. If we can do our best to create our intentions, thoughts, and agreements mindfully and through the lens of our authentic truth, this leaves us with less work to do moving forward.

Becoming very self-aware and conscious of our internal landscape is a skill that takes cultivation and practice, but it can allow us to stop any limiting intentions in their tracks before they impact us in harmful ways. If we become aware of thoughts we might be having about ourselves or others that are negative or diminishing in some way, we can consciously choose to stop those thoughts in their tracks. We can also choose to destroy any negative thoughtforms or structures formed by limiting intentions if we suspect we might have created them. Imagine them dissolving or burning up into ashes and this will do the trick.

We can also ask our guides to help us destroy any energetic structures we have created through our own limiting intentions. These could be contracts, curses, or other intentions that impact us or other people negatively. In some cases, we may need to specifically identify and work through limiting intentions we have created, but in others, we can clear any unintentional harm we have done with our intentions by giving permission. You could say something like:

Guides, higher self, and Spirit, I give permission to destroy any limiting thoughtforms, contracts, curses, or other limiting intentions that I have created that are harming myself or others. Please clear these energies and any other energies that have resulted from their presence in a way that is in my highest good and the highest good of all creation.

We can also be mindful about the agreements, connections, and contracts we make. Before making an agreement, spend some time journaling about what your intentions are, why you want to enter the agreement, and what you suspect the intentions of the other person or institution might be. If we get really honest about our intentions, we can often stop ourselves from entering into toxic agreements before they have an impact on our lives.

Learning to look under the surface when it comes to the intentions of other people is very helpful as well. People often say things that they want us to hear rather than what they are really feeling or intending. Tuning into our intuition, body, and heart can give us the clues we need to see through the illusion and cut through to the truth of any matter.

One of the most powerful practices I have learned from my guides is to always intuitively look at a representation of the energy behind a circumstance, person, or object to gain a more clear understanding. We might hear the words, "I only want the best for you," from someone we are connected to, but if we intend to view a representation of the energy behind these words intuitively, we might see brown, dark red, or black energy swirling around chaotically. If we intend to feel the intention of the words intuitively, we may feel tense, anxious, or nauseous in our body. It's important to look beyond the face value of our experiences to truly understand the intentions that create our reality. Two physically identical objects or experiences can have very different energy that create both of them. It is always the energy that matters most, so it's important to look at the energy first.

It can also be helpful to reflect on any existing physical agreements you might have in your life and the energy that might be behind those. Look at bank accounts, insurance agreements, healthcare providers, educational institutions, your workplace, and any other areas of your life where you have agreements. Are these agreements and contracts you have in alignment with your values? Do a little research and make sure the people, places, and institutions you invest your energy in have values that are in alignment with yours.

You may find that the bank you keep your money in funds another organization that you feel does harm to yourself or others. If your money is in that bank, on some level you are financially supporting the exact thing that is doing harm. In this case, you might decide to move your assets to a credit union or member-supported bank. This might seem inconsequential, but being intentional about our connections and contracts in our physical lives can have a very significant impact on cleaning up our energy.

Learning to see life through the lens of intention and energy can take some work. We are so wired to believe only what we see, that we often get ourselves into trouble when we can't look beyond the face value of our experiences. The more we practice this skill and use it each day in all of our interactions, the more innate and automatic it will become. Life is a lot easier when we can see the truth of things and act accordingly.

Of course, we aren't perfect and we often see life through the lens of our traumas and limiting beliefs. This can cause us to act out of shadow aspects of ourselves and circumvent the truth until those parts of us receive the love and healing that they need. We can also choose to turn a blind eye to the harmful intentions of others when we feel what they offer us is needed for one reason or another. The more healing work we do, though, the less we are likely to be affected by limiting intentions, and the more we free ourselves from blocks to our personal sovereignty.

Part 3

Exploring Ancestral Gifts
and Connections

Chapter 7

Ancestral Blessings

As challenging as the impact of the burdens in our Ancestral Blueprint can be, our ancestral inheritances are not limited to the hardships we experience. There are beautiful gifts and exceptional wisdom that are accessible to us through our Ancestral Blueprint. These assets are the direct result of balanced energies and mastery of experience inherited through our genetic and soul lineages.

Our bodies are physically formed through the DNA of our genetic ancestors. They give us life, and they allow us to move, interact, and create in ways that are unique to each of us. Our inherited physical features can allow us to do the many activities that we love to do, and when we are gifted with certain physical strengths, this can allow us to do these activities even better. Our bodies also allow us to express soul gifts physically. Our soul's aptitudes can only be accessed and expressed if our physical body is capable of doing so, and it is our genetic inheritances that create the opportunity for us to embody our unique soul gifts and wisdom.

The same is true for our convictions. There are always ways

that our soul and our genetic lineage deviate from limiting and toxic patterns that we find systemically in our culture. Acting and viewing the world through balanced beliefs that come through our ancestral lines can be a great catalyst for positive change, both within our own Ancestral Blueprint and the world we live in. The more we embody beliefs that encourage tolerance, love, and acceptance of self and others, the more these sentiments spread to future generations. This is how change happens, and it starts with anchoring the balanced aspects of our Ancestral Blueprint into our personal expression.

We can also inherit a very loving and balanced way of behaving through both our genetic and soul lineages. If we have a strong disposition as a soul toward certain behaviors, that strength in character can bring balance to a genetic lineage that may be lacking in certain areas. The same is true for balanced behaviors in our genetic lineage that may teach us a more optimal way of being. We have many opportunities to change our behavior and behavioral patterns in our lineage for the better when we access the healed energies in our Ancestral Blueprint. It is our positive intentions and our ability to act through them that allow us to break toxic cycles and begin healing the wounds caused by them.

These gifts that we inherit through our Ancestral Blueprint are ancestral blessings. These blessings come in the form of the connections we have through our Ancestral Blueprint, as well as the soul and genetic skills and wisdom we have access to in each lifetime. These ancestral blessings contain everything we need to balance the ancestral burdens in our Ancestral Blueprint. Just as we can work with our ancestral burdens on an energetic level, we can also work with our ancestral blessings energetically to bring great healing and balance to our lineages. For every challenge we face, there is always a balanced resolution that we have access to, and our ancestral blessings are a perfect place to begin looking for support and healing.

HEALING WITH ANCESTRAL CONNECTIONS

Our ancestral connections are a powerful resource that we can tap into in very active ways. We have already explored how we can work with our ancestral guides and our spiritual support team to balance the energies in our Ancestral Blueprint once we meet the prerequisites for healing. Actively employing this relationship with our spiritual support team is perhaps the most powerful way to accelerate healing and personal growth. When we choose to actively partner with Spirit and trust the guidance we receive, we know that we never have to travel alone and we are always led forward in ways that are in alignment with our most positive potential.

Ancestral guides are just one part of the picture, though. Perhaps the most powerful connection that we have in our lineage is our own self. Our soul lineage contains every past version of ourselves, and while we are at our most advanced stage of growth as a soul with each moment we experience, many of our past selves have gifts and healing that they can share with us to help us on our path.

Working with some of our more balanced past selves can open many doors for us when it comes to activating our Ancestral Blueprint in positive ways. Life goes in cycles, and while we may have had a very balanced life thousands of years ago, subsequent traumas and limiting experiences can and often do disturb former balance. We can work with other versions of ourselves to intentionally and multidimensionally reclaim balance within our soul's energy stream where it has been lost.

You can begin this work by finding a quiet place to sit, meditate, and receive healing. Once you are comfortable, close your eyes and take a few deep breaths to relax your mind and body. Now, extend your palms face up in front of you, and when you feel ready, call a balanced alternate version of yourself forward to connect with you. You do not need to know who they are or what point in time they come from for this exercise to work. Your intention is enough to bring this version of you forth, as you are always connected to your own self through your Ancestral Blueprint and soul energies regardless of your awareness. You can speak something similar to the following out loud or in your mind:

> *I call forth a version of myself that is in my highest good to connect with now to join me in an exercise to balance the energies in my soul energy stream. Please take my hands and connect with me.*

Your alternate self will immediately come forth and take your hands. Take a few moments here to feel their energy and you can close your eyes and picture them if you would like to. Does it feel different than your energy does? What sensations do you feel in your body?

Once you have connected with your alternate self, with your intention you can balance any energies that have become out of balance through any of your lifetimes that have occurred between yourself and this version of you, as long as it is in your highest good to do so. You can do this by speaking something like the following out loud or in your mind:

> *I clear my blood from me to you. I clear my bones from me to you. I clear my DNA from me to you. I clear my energy stream from me to you. I release all trauma energy, emotional energy, limiting beliefs, limiting programs, limiting intentions, and limiting connections from me to you that are in my highest good to release at this time.*

With this statement complete, allow the energies that are

ready to clear to release from your body and energy field. You will only release what is in your best interest to release at this time.

Next, you will ask your alternate self to attune you to the balanced templates and energies available to you through your soul lineage energy stream. You can do so with a statement like the following:

I now ask that my energy body and Ancestral Blueprint be attuned to the balanced energies available to me through my soul lineage energy stream. Please bless me with any energies and healed templates that are in my highest good to receive at this time.

Allow yourself to receive these energies, and when you feel the healing is complete, thank your alternate self for working with you and do your post-healing self-care routine.

This is a beautifully simple exercise that can have some very profound effects and meets all of the healing prerequisites. We can name what is real within our energy field by listing the energies that we would like to clear. We identify the origin of these imbalances by recognizing that they occurred sometime in our existence between ourselves and this particular alternate self. We understand the effect that these energies are having because we know that they are creating imbalance in our lives, and we can additionally feel the contrast between our own energy and the energy of the alternate self we are working with. Finally, knowing how we want to shift things is as simple as knowing that we want to balance the imbalance and release these dense energies.

This healing allows us to clear energies from past experiences that may have been difficult for us to access or identify otherwise, and this same process can be used to heal other facets of your Ancestral Blueprint. You can repeat this healing by calling forth a different alternate self that may have other balanced energies for you to work with, or you can work with the same aspect of yourself again in the future as you grow and become ready to release additional energies.

You can also repeat this same exercise with a focus on your genetic lineage. The process is exactly the same, except this time you will call forth one of your genetic ancestral guides to connect with you. You may be general and ask for any ancestral guide that is in your highest good to work with to come forward, or you may be specific and call forth a guide from a specific aspect of your genetic lineage. You may say something like:

I call forth an ancestral guide from my mother's father's line of my genetic lineage that is in my highest good to connect with now to join me in an exercise to balance the energies in my genetic energy stream. Please take my hands and connect with me.

Once your ancestral guide is called forth, repeat the clearing statement and make note of how you feel as these energies clear.

It can be helpful to journal about any shifts that you notice in yourself in the following days and weeks after performing this healing. You may notice feeling lighter after the energies have fully cleared, you may notice shifts in your thoughts and emotions, you may notice that certain challenges begin to resolve for you, and you may even notice yourself being drawn to learn new interests or activities.

Working with the connections we have through our Ancestral Blueprint is multidimensional healing work. When we can think beyond our physical linear experience, this multidimensional awareness alone gives us access to new levels of healing and growth. No matter how challenging or limiting our ancestral burdens might be for us, there are always healed and loving connections somewhere in our lineage. Ancestral Blueprint work allows us to reach across time to access the loving connections that we may be lacking in our physical lives, and it gives us a new appreciation and love for ourselves as an eternal being.

✌
EMBODYING SOUL SKILLS AND WISDOM

Beyond activating and working with our uplifting ancestral connections, we can also work with our other ancestral blessings in multidimensional ways. Our soul skills and wisdom are the result of all of the balanced energies and growth we have achieved through our experiences as a soul, and these energies are permanently encoded into our soul lineage energy stream. Regardless of whether we are able to embody these energies in our physical lives or not, they do exist and we can access them to some degree.

Often the ancestral burdens that come from the genetic aspect of our Ancestral Blueprint block our soul's balanced energies from expressing. This includes belief templates that are balanced and reflective of our core truth, soul wisdom and knowledge that we have gained, certain skills and aptitudes that we have as a soul, and other unique energies that belong to us. We often have difficulty executing our soul mission here or taking action toward living our purpose because of the genetic ancestral blocks that we have to grapple with first.

Luckily, we can use our awareness of the two different aspects of our Ancestral Blueprint to release large amounts of energy that are not in alignment with our soul-self and all of the balance, wisdom, and growth we have achieved throughout our lifetimes. Before performing this exercise, be aware that it can lead to a very significant energetic release that can last for many days. It is important to be prepared for this release, and to be aware that you will never be permitted by your higher self to release anything that is not in your highest good to release at a given time.

The first step of this healing is to find a quiet and comfortable place to be with yourself and Spirit. When you feel ready to begin the healing, close your eyes and call forth your spiritual support team to assist you. You can say something like:

I call upon my guides, higher self, and Spirit to assist me in this healing to release myself from ancestral burdens that prevent me from expressing my authentic and balanced soul energies, soul skills, and soul wisdom.

Once you have called forth your spiritual support team, your next step is to bring your awareness to the understanding that while your soul energies may currently be blocked by genetic ancestral burdens, as a sovereign being with free will, you can always choose to remove these blocks and express more of yourself. With this awareness in mind, you can now request that Spirit assist you in clearing any energies from the genetic lineage aspect of your Ancestral Blueprint that are not in alignment with your balanced soul energies. You can do this with a statement similar to the following:

I give permission to my guides, higher self, and Spirit to clear any emotional energies, trauma energies, limiting beliefs, limiting programs, limiting contracts, curses, other limiting intentions, and all other limiting energies that are not in alignment with my physical embodiment of the balanced energies in my soul lineage energy stream. I give permission for this clearing to commence in a way that serves my highest good and the highest good of all creation.

You will likely feel energy begin to clear once you complete this statement. Sit with the release for as long as you feel called to. When you feel ready for the next step, you will continue by giving your spiritual support team permission to replace any energies that have been removed from your Ancestral Blueprint and energy body with energies from your soul lineage that are balanced. You can do this with a statement similar to the following:

I give permission to my guides, higher self, and Spirit to replace any cleared energies with templates and energies from my soul lineage that are in alignment with my core truth and are in my highest good to receive at this time.

Once this step is complete, thank your spiritual support team for their assistance. The healing will continue for several hours or days until it is complete, but you can go about your life while this process occurs. Spirit will facilitate the release, and it is your job to make sure you take care of yourself and get plenty of rest. Make sure to check in with yourself and your body each day. You may feel unusually tired, emotional, or sore as this release occurs, but know that these are temporary side effects of a very powerful and positive healing process.

This exercise teaches us that the blocks, patterns, and limitations that we experience in life are only able to exist because we are either not aware of them, or do not understand that we have the power to change things for the better. This healing offers us a profound opportunity to not only bring more balance and upliftment into our own lives, but to also offer our balanced soul energies as a gift to our genetic lineage. Once this healing is complete, the work we have done within our own Ancestral Blueprint becomes available to our genetic lineage and those who would like to receive this healing for themselves.

༙

THE EMOTIONAL COMPASS

Unfortunately, as a society, we tend to chase good feelings in a very unhealthy way. We do whatever it takes to feel good, even if it's only for a moment, and we think that something is wrong with us if the tides suddenly turn and we start to feel anxious or low. We do our very best to avoid feeling anything less than good, and this frequently leads to emotional repression.

Our emotions are a compass. They guide us to our ancestral burdens. They show us when we are in alignment with our core truth and when we are not. If we feel anxious, sad, angry, jealous, disappointed, frustrated, or any other emotion we consider less than optimal, we are being guided to an ancestral burden. Our lower emotions tell us when trauma energy is being activated within our Ancestral Blueprint, when we are looking through the lens of a limiting belief, or when we are being influenced by a limiting intention. The more we avoid and repress our emotions, the more we waste the valuable tools that they are for guiding us toward the imbalances that we desperately desire to transform.

We often blame our emotions for our troubles, but this is like being lost in a forest and blaming our map because we refuse to use it. We think things would be better if we could just feel better. The truth is, our emotions are a side effect, not a cause. We feel better when we balance the imbalances that create our emotions in the first place. Our body is a finely tuned instrument that knows exactly how to tell us when something is out of balance. It generates emotional energy and then physical sensations so that we can feel this energy when it wants to tell us something important. We have forgotten how to work with this instrument, though, and instead of recognizing the imbalances that our emotions are trying to guide us to, we tell our body that it's wrong or that we don't want to listen.

While our lower emotions guide us to the imbalances in our Ancestral Blueprint, our more uplifting emotions can tell us when we are operating from our most authentic expression. The caveat is that for this to be true, we must be feeling these uplifting emotions naturally and when our nervous system is regulated for them to truly show us when we are on the right track. Humans have all sorts of ways to feel a false sense of upliftment through addictive substances, dissociative behaviors, and avoidance tactics. When we chase good feelings through any method that is meant to circumvent the imbalances we haven't faced yet, we are actually creating more imbalance in our Ancestral Blueprint. The only true way to upliftment and positive transformation is to move through all of the things from our past and our ancestors' past that we haven't yet looked at. We have to look at and feel it all, the good and the bad, the uplifting and the depressing, the beautiful and the horrific.

When we begin to surrender to our emotions and get comfortable with being uncomfortable, we can use them for the beautiful gift that they are to guide us to the imbalances in our Ancestral Blueprint. When we experience a lower emotion, this is an indicator that an experience we are having is in resonance with something from our past. What we feel is the energy of all of the repressed emotions from every similar experience we have ever had all the way back to the original trauma that created an imbalance for us. If we can identify the original trauma or a resulting limiting pattern or intention, we can clear all of that dense energy that has been anchored into our being, including the trapped emotional energy that has been activated through the experience.

The key to using our emotions as a compass is to try our very best to not act through our emotions, and then recognize that they are present and mindfully work through them. When we identify an emotional sensation we are feeling that is uncomfortable, we can ask ourselves a series of questions to get to the root of it. When have I felt like this before in my life? What does the experience that is causing me to feel this way have in common with other experiences I've had in the past? Are there any themes here that remind me of a past trauma? You can ask your spiritual support team to assist you with this self-reflection process and to help you recall any memories or patterns that might help guide you forward. Once you identify any ancestral burdens that this emotion is guiding you to, you can work through any of the exercises in this book to release what you have discovered.

If we experience uncomfortable or lower emotions in the present, we are being guided to something from our past. If we have an experience and there is nothing from our own past or our lineage's past out of balance related to the experience, we will not feel lower emotions and we will not be triggered. We can shrug it off, send love, and move on with our day without a second thought.

If an experience does trigger lower emotions, we are being shown that the experience is in resonance with something in our energy field that needs some attention. That something may be from our own life, from a past life, or from a genetic ances-tor's experience, but there is something to look at just the same. We never attract challenging experiences to us unless there is something in our energy field in resonance with that experience, so we can use our challenges as a tool to work toward positive transformation rather than becoming a victim of our negative experiences.

Mindfully using our emotions as a compass is one of the most powerful tools that we have as humans to identify the imbalances in our Ancestral Blueprint, but only as long as we honor them and use them properly. When those feelings pop up, they are there for a reason and it is our choice whether we repress them or use them to guide us forward.

Working to balance our ancestral burdens cultivates balance

in our entire being. Once we achieve balance, we no longer need our lower emotions to point us to anything hidden and they fall away. As a consequence of our healing, we then experience uplifting emotions and positive experiences that reflect balance.

THE GIFT OF OUR BURDENS

It's very easy for us humans to cherish the things that make us feel good and to place great value on what we think are the most admirable aspects of our Ancestral Blueprint. We direct attention to our skills and wisdom, while simultaneously hiding the burdens that plague us from others and even ourselves. We feel shame about our ancestral burdens even though they are an integral part of our experience.

The truth is, our ancestral burdens are often our greatest ancestral blessing of all. The process of alchemizing our ancestral burdens is what forges our ancestral blessings. Our soul skills and wisdom are a direct result of navigating and balancing ancestral burdens and the challenges that we inherit from our lineage. Without challenges and the desire to overcome our challenges, we are often content with the status quo, which is not a state that fosters growth. We can't learn and grow if we can't embrace change.

Humans do have a penchant for growing comfortable in very uncomfortable situations. Our minds tell us that the devil we know is better than the devil we don't know, but what if there is no devil at all and we are really just living on a spectrum of change that is completely in our control to navigate? Maybe we've just forgotten that we have the power to change things for the better because we come from a long line of ancestors who have been locked into the impact of ancestral burdens for generations.

Ancestral burdens take work to overcome, but they do promote change and growth when we consciously choose to work through them. They also promote change when we cast them aside and ignore their impact, but this is change that can leave our lives looking very grim. Change is inevitable, but we do have the power to encourage change in one way or the other. We are not powerless victims of change unless we choose to look away from the past. When we begin shining a light on our ancestral burdens, we unearth the ancestral memory of our role as sovereign creators of our lives. This is a gift that is priceless beyond all else.

Chapter 8
Claiming The Future

Healing is difficult no matter how we approach it, but it can be far more challenging when we don't have the tools or the awareness we need to overcome our burdens in life. While awareness of the imbalances in ourselves and our lineage is an important first step, it is not enough to heal. Yet, awareness of our imbalances is often all we strive for. We spend decades in therapy trying to learn to identify our emotions and patterns. We are often shocked that something from our childhood could so deeply impact our present experience. We often look only at the mind or emotions and neglect our bodies, energy, and spirit. We often hold on to unhealthy habits, circumstances, and relationships with an iron grip and hope that something external to ourselves will finally change things for the better. We learn to cope.

This is certainly no fault of our own. Our modern society has forgotten the ancient wisdom of our ancestors that tells us there is another way. Our ancient ancestors wait patiently, guiding us in our dreams, waiting for us to hear their call. They sprinkle breadcrumbs in front of us, hoping we will follow them home. We do the best we can with what we are taught, and it often takes a catalyzing experience to wake us up enough to see that there is something more to our story than the bullet points on our resumé.

While we may have forgotten much of the wisdom of our ancestors, this wisdom can never truly be lost, as it is encoded within our unique Ancestral Blueprint. Ancestral wisdom lives in the multidimensional layers of energy that make us who and what we are. This knowledge is all there waiting to be reclaimed. By consciously embodying more of our soul-self, we start to bring this knowledge out of the shadows and into our conscious awareness. This is an important step in our own personal transformation journey and for the planet as a whole.

When we work within our Ancestral Blueprint, we become the physical embodiment of conscious transformation in our lineage. In doing this work, we can truly alchemize all that is out of balance in our experience through our energy-first way of seeing the world. We become the programmers of our lives. We hack the system and we become masters of manifestation and transformation - we become alchemists. Our lives take shape around our authentic expression, and we begin to live the life we have desired for so long.

This sounds like a beautiful process, but despite its beauty, it is not without hardship. We have to look backward to move forward, and looking back can bring up many things that are difficult to see and painful to feel. This work is never easy. When we suddenly become aware of all of the unsavory things that need healing in our Ancestral Blueprint, we have picked up a torch for our lineage that may have been dropped thousands of years ago. We have a lot of work to do to balance the backlog of ancestral burdens that past generations have collected and left untouched. This is work that can be done, but it also means that we have to see, feel, and understand many difficult things. This is a fruitful process that often doesn't look or feel good while we are in the throws of it.

As humans, we love to think we are working toward a set goal or a certain event, but this work has no end. There are beautiful blessings that we can experience while doing Ancestral Blueprint work, but there is always work to be done. This is not a task for weeks, months, or years, it is a task for a lifetime - lifetimes even. When we embark on this healing journey, we have to make peace with the journey itself. This journey will always be a foundational part of our lives as long as we continue to choose the path of growth and healing.

This work takes emotional fortitude and dedication. It takes a deep and unbreakable trust that something bigger than ourselves is leading us to a better existence, even when we feel like we are lost in a dark abyss. The only way out is through, and through can test us in unthinkable ways.

BRINGERS OF CHANGE

Many of us have entered into our genetic lineage because we are the bringers of change. We are here to end a cycle, and the only way to do this is to introduce something different. We might be that "something different" for our genetic lineage. Likewise, our genetic lineage can be that "something different" for us. This can sometimes leave us feeling out of place when we are among certain family members. We may hold different beliefs, convictions, interests, and attitudes than those who raised us, and this can feel difficult and challenging at times.

In other cases, we may have followed the path laid out for us by the generations that came before us, only to realize that this path is causing us pain and suffering. We wake up one day and know in our bones that we can no longer continue down this path that is not in alignment with our heart's vision and is crushing our soul. We change course, willing to endure whatever consequences our choice to change may have. As we awaken to our soul's commitment to this work, we suddenly begin to care more about our own well-being and happiness than meeting the expectations of others. We feel more free.

I'm here to tell you that if you feel very different from those who brought you into this life, there is likely a very good reason for it - even if these differences have created challenge, conflict, and trauma for you. It may very well be that you have the gifts that are so greatly needed to repair what has been fractured in the genetic lineage you have incarnated into, and that your genetic lineage has gifts for you that are meant to spark soul growth and remembrance. It may be that the soul blessings you have brought with you are so innate to who you are and so unshakable that they have not only been able to survive your exposure to entrenched imbalance, but are the medicine needed to balance your Ancestral Blueprint. You may be here to stop the progression of trauma through your lineage in its tracks, for the benefit of yourself and future generations.

We often have to experience the same trauma patterns as our ancestors in order to understand them enough to create the change that is so needed. What makes us different from others is that at some point, we are able to snap out of the victim and blame mentality that so often accompanies generational trauma. We get fed up, we say no more, we start to take responsibility for our experience, and we begin to awaken a fire within ourselves. Our guides, higher self, and Spirit stoke the flames and we become increasingly unwilling to travel down the same road as those who have come before us. We stop dead in our tracks and we begin to look for answers.

If we feel called to this work, some part of ourselves is telling us that we are ready to begin this journey. Our journey will be unique to us and will take as much time as it needs to, but it is a journey that we are prepared for. We are ready when we are ready, and not a moment sooner. When we make the choice to heal, we are always guided to the resources, information, and support we need when the time is right.

There are many outcomes of Ancestral Blueprint work that are as varied as the work itself. We may never get the validation we have sought from our family our entire life, or we may have surprising and uplifting changes in our familial relationships. Certain family members may never choose to change or heal, or they may make giant leaps forward as we do our own internal work. We may have to permanently sever certain toxic relationships, or our relational bonds could be strengthened beyond belief. Whatever the outcome, it is exactly as it is meant to be. The work we do within ourselves effectively transforms toxic ancestral patterns. We just have to let the chips fall where they may in the aftermath of this transformation.

When we transform energy on this primal level of our being, things change. It is inevitable. Although change is what we desire when we embark on this journey, we cannot control all of the things that change and we must be prepared for loss. We may be ready to lose the unhealthy patterns that limit us, but are we ready to lose the people and circumstances in our lives that are not ready or are unwilling to change with us? This is something that can and will happen as we heal, and it is difficult and painful.

Not everyone will be able to come on the journey with us, and with loss comes grief. Even if we so desperately want change, it is important to grieve what we have left behind. We can't move forward until we fully grieve what we feel we have lost, even if what we have lost was always just an illusion. With loss we make room for something new, and the things that we have had to let go of will always find us in a new, more balanced form. We let go of toxic connections to receive new uplifting connections. We let go of our false identity to embody our true identity. We let go of our base desires to receive what our heart desires. We let go of the past to create a better future, but only after witnessing and transforming everything out of balance in our being.

ᴥ

EMBRACING YOUR LINEAGE

It is very easy for us to identify as a victim. The traumas and abuses we have suffered and that our ancestors have suffered shape much of our experience. If we are only able to identify with the victims in our lineage, though, we miss the whole picture and we reject important parts of our past.

When we have imbalance in our Ancestral Blueprint, we will often find that opposing archetypes also exist within our lineage and our own self. If there is victimization, there is always a victimizer. If there is oppression, there is always an oppressor. If there is submission, there is always domination. Where one exists, so does the other. We cannot balance this polarity unless we witness, understand, and make peace with both sides of the coin. We are impacted energetically and physically by the experiences and actions of *all* our ancestors - regardless of which side of the coin they embodied. When there is imbalance, both of the polarized potentials of the archetypes we see in our lineage exist somewhere within our Ancestral Blueprint and within us.

How these imbalances manifest for us in our own lives often comes down to the influences of our soul energies. If we have a predisposition as a soul toward abuse, control, or domination, we may express this physically if this archetype exists within our genetic lineage. If we have a predisposition toward victimization or submission, we may express this physically instead.

Where one polarity exists within us, though, the other always exists too. Even if we physically express certain imbalances in our actions, we often express the opposite imbalance within ourselves internally. If abuse runs in our lineage, we might become a victim in our external reality in many ways as we attract experiences through the traumas in our Ancestral Blueprint. If we embody the victim physically, somewhere in us is an abuser as well. In this case, we might find that we abuse ourselves in many ways with negative self-talk, self-harm, substance abuse, neglect of our basic needs, and countless other ways. Where there is a victim, there is always a victimizer, and we have to look at both within ourselves to begin to truly heal the parts of us that have been fractured by ancestral trauma. We pride ourselves on not behaving in the same ways as those who hurt us, yet we are often harming ourselves in hidden ways. This is not balanced, and it is certainly not the truth of who we are.

It is important to be mindful of the archetypes that we identify with when doing ancestral healing work and exploring the traumas in our lineage. If we identify too heavily with some-thing, it is likely that we are turning a blind eye to its opposite within us. Usually, the things that we have the most aversion to live within us somewhere in some form. We have to be willing to look at all parts of ourselves, especially the parts that we keep secret and hidden, to truly master Ancestral Blueprint work.

We also have to be willing to forgive ourselves when the time is right for all of the ways we have abandoned our true nature. We all have imbalances that follow us into this life. We act through them, we choose through them, we believe through them, and we feel through them. This is part of life and it is something that we all have to come to terms with as part of our healing process. When we forgive ourselves for acting in harmful ways, we open the door to something different. If we blame ourselves for the limitations of our past, we lock ourselves into those patterns. This is the way the Ancestral Blue-print works. Imbalance begets imbalance, and we can only change it if we choose something more loving for ourselves.

We may also find as we do this work that we feel drawn to certain cultures, traditions, and spiritual practices that don't seem to quite fit into what we know about our genetic ancestry. I have studied practices from many cultures and traditions in my own journey. I have found that when something truly resonates with us, regardless of the avenue or tradition it comes to us through, there is something there that we need for our healing. Likewise, if a practice or practitioner makes us feel uneasy, unwell, or hesitant, even if it appears on the surface to be aligned with our tradition or beliefs, there is likely a reason we should run the other way.

Truth is truth, regardless of what shape it takes, what culture it comes through, what rituals it is expressed through, or what words are used to express it. There is a reason that nearly all spiritual traditions from around the world contain similar stories, similar concepts, and similar understandings of the nature of the universe. All traditions contain some element of universal truth, and all traditions contain some element of fiction, fantasy, or calculated lies. They are often a mix of truth and manipulation of truth, and it takes some practice to discern the difference in many cases. This is why it is so important to follow our own inner truth rather than follow a set of ideals prescribed by someone else.

Truth is something we can feel in our body, our bones, and our heart. It is not something that we interpret with our minds. Our truth belongs to us, and no one else can tell us what that truth is, no matter how hard they may try. The more we work with our Ancestral Blueprint, the more we will uncover our own unique truth.

Do not be afraid of your truth. Do not reject your truth because it is different from what you have been told by others. Do not allow yourself to be enticed by the comfort of familiarity when that familiarity is not aligned with your soul-self. Above all things, trust yourself as you navigate your Ancestral Blueprint and the potential it holds within it. You may experience a backlash or rejection from those who witness and feel challenged by your truth and your authenticity, but if you stay the course, you will find the people who will embrace all of who you are.

THE BLOOMING

Sovereignty is innate. It is our divine right as a living being. Unfortunately, this is wisdom we have forgotten, and this forgetting has allowed us to be enslaved by the burdens of the past. When we don't remember we are free, it's easy to convince us and the rest of humanity otherwise. As we transform our Ancestral Blueprint, we reclaim our freedom. We no longer play by rules that our social structures expect us to play by, and we attract something completely different from what we have known before. We live through the truth of our soul-self rather than a construct built to limit us in countless ways. The more we free ourselves, the more we can embrace and embody our purpose in this life. We feel the joy and fulfillment of being in alignment with our unique role in the human collective, and we inspire others with the light we have awakened in ourselves.

The more we walk down this path of ancestral healing, the more we realize that not everything is as it appears on the surface. We may find that we have unexpected ancestral connections, or that we have had unexpected experiences in other lifetimes. The more we explore ourselves through our past, we begin to see that our beliefs about who we are reflect a significant amount of cultural dogma that may not be our truth at all.

As we each awaken and bring forth the ancient seeds of ancestral knowledge within us, our connections are strengthened with those who came before us. We begin to see in ways we couldn't see in the past. We begin to dream a new future into existence. We begin to hear the whispers of the Ancient Ones as they call us forth into the unknown.

The strength that comes from healing our roots allows for a great blooming within us. We open in ways we never thought possible. We try things that we never thought we could. We have exciting experiences that we always thought were for someone else, but never us. Our relationships uplift us, our work becomes supportive and fulfilling, our life opens up, and we experience peace.

The blooming can take getting used to. When we are accustomed to limitation and struggle, it is hard to imagine something different. When all we have ever known is the crushing weight of trauma, conflict, and challenge, it can be very difficult to trust that something else is out there for us. There is an initial shock that can run through our bodies when we start to experience true joy. We may even fear feeling that joy, lest the prize be taken away after getting a small taste of it. The prize isn't going anywhere though. It will wait until we are ready to embrace it.

When our ancestors call us forth as the healers of our lineage, we are always met with grace, patience, and unconditional love. This is not a one-sided mission, and it is not the mission of a martyr, though it can feel that way sometimes. Speaking from experience, I can say that any suffering we endure as we heal pales in comparison to the gifts that lie on the other side of that healing. When we trust our heart rather than our mind and our programming, we can always find the path out of the darkness and into the light.

When we answer the call of our ancestors, we heal and we grow. We free our lineage from the grip of trauma. We birth a new life for ourselves and humanity from the seeds of sovereignty that we have planted and cultivated ourselves. With each day that we reclaim our roots, we free ourselves from the limitations of our past and call into being a beautiful future that is born from the dreams of our ancestors.

❧

May you know the wisdom of your ancestors
and embody the truth of your soul
to uplift yourself and humanity
for the highest good of all.

Have you enjoyed this book?

Pay it forward and help other readers find the healing offerings shared in this book by leaving a review on the site where you purchased it.

About the Author

Kristen Blythe, founder of Rooted Wisdom Holistic Life Coaching, is an intuitive coach and energy healing teacher with over 20 years of experience in the field of energy medicine. She is the creator of the ROESA Method™ healing framework, and is a Reiki Master Teacher, certified meditation instructor, and has trained in a multitude of healing modalities and metaphysical practices throughout her career. Her grounded approach to spirituality and healing is highly acclaimed and is designed to be accessible to all, regardless of background or experience. Her passion is empowering individuals as their own self-healers and showing others how they can transform in miraculous ways by deeply connecting with themselves and Spirit.

For more from Kristen Blythe, visit:
www.rootedwisdomcoaching.com

Made in the USA
Middletown, DE
30 August 2023

37462032R00097